THREE TO GET READY

THREE TO GET READY

A GUIDE FOR THE ENGAGED

BY

JOHN G. QUESNELL
A . C . S . W .

THE LITURGICAL PRESS

COLLEGEVILLE, MINNESOTA

Photo credits:

James C. Clark, p. xviii, Leo Kim, p. 53, Jerry Morgenroth, pp. 96, 152.

Cover by Brother Placid, O.S.B.

DEDICATION

*The staff of the
St. Paul Catholic Youth Center*

CONTENTS

ACKNOWLEDGEMENTS ix

FOREWORD xi

INTRODUCTION xiii

SECTION I —
  ENGAGEMENT: A TIME FOR KNOWING
  ME, YOU, AND GOD
    Chapter 1 — Love Is Patient and Kind . . . 1
    Chapter 2 — Love Is Not Ill-Mannered . . . 8
    Chapter 3 — The Cold Pricklies 12
    Chapter 4 — Love Does Not Keep A
                Record of Wrongs 17
    Chapter 5 — My Way Is My Way 22
    Chapter 6 — Me and My Foibles 30

SECTION II —
  THAT THE TWO SHALL BECOME ONE
    Chapter 7 — From Woman's Lib To Adam's Rib 54
    Chapter 8 — Why Male and Female . . . 64
    Chapter 9 — The IT'S and DIS of Marriage . 70
    Chapter 10 — Money Matters in Marriage . . 81

SECTION III —
  MALE AND FEMALE HE CREATED THEM
    Chapter 11 — Adam Knew Eve 97
    Chapter 12 — Technological Triumph? . . . 110
    Chapter 13 — Technological Travesty . . . 112
    Chapter 14 — Why Wait? 118
    Chapter 15 — The Devolution 127
    Chapter 16 — Understanding God's Will . . 131
    Chapter 17 — The Honeymoon 142

SECTION IV —
  BUILDING UPON ROCK
    Chapter 18 — Jesus As Lord 153

ACKNOWLEDGEMENTS

I am deeply indebted to all those who have influenced me during the past several years and who have helped me develop the ideas conveyed in this book. Certainly the thousands of engaged couples whom I have met in programs conducted at the Catholic Youth Centers in St. Paul, MN, and Fargo, ND, and at St. Olaf's Church in downtown Minneapolis have provided the impetus for developing these ideas. I am grateful to Fathers Michael Kolar, David McCauley, Grover Diemert, and Francis Fleming, and Mr. Louis Grams for the opportunity to participate in these programs.

My thanks to Fr. Paul Marx, O.S.B., director of the Human Life Center, St. John's University, Collegeville, MN, and to Fr. James Materi, O.M.I., editor of *Our Family*, for their encouragement.

Fathers Francis Kittock and Richard Villano were kind enough to critique the entire manuscript. There is no way to adequately thank friends who contributed such help. I am also grateful to Fr. George Freeman, Msgr. Jerome Quinn, Fr. Mark Dosh, Mrs. Bob Nevin, Mr. Wayne Hergott, Mr. and Mrs. Harry Miller, Roger and Peg Carter, and Don and Sylvia Kramer who critiqued certain parts of the manuscript. The retreats for the engaged gave me the opportunity to associate with Mr. Robert Labat, Mrs. Bea Rystad, and Tom and Barb Fischer, whose ideas and suggestions were very helpful in developing the chapter on finances.

During the past several years, the full-time and volunteer staff of the St. Paul Catholic Youth Center has been extremely helpful. Their insights and inspiration strengthen the message of *Three to Get Ready*. The sisters of the Cenacle in Wayzata, MN, have provided inspiration and encouragement for which I am grateful.

I am very grateful to my colleague Dr. John Haas and our office staff. I cannot adequately thank Mrs. Linda Hanson, who not only assumed full responsibility for typing the manuscript but who also helped critique and edit it.

I am grateful to Fides Publishers for permitting me to use some content from *Marriage: A Discovery Together* that was applicable to engaged as well as married couples.

Finally, I must thank my family who actively helped prepare the manuscript. Our daughter Cathy thought of the title, suggested a theme for the cover, and ran many necessary errands. Our sons Mike and Tim were kind enough to stay out of her hair while she was working. My wife Alice helped critique and edit the manuscript and develop the ideas and suggestions contained within *Three to Get Ready*. I am truly fortunate to have received the gift of a good wife.

John G. Quesnell

FOREWORD

What is obvious after reading just a few pages of this book is that the author has a "bias" regarding marriage — he believes that it can be a most productive style of life, provided the couple puts into it a little "work" and lots of real love, not love as our contemporary society defines it, but as St. Paul talks about it in 1 Corinthians 13:1-13. *Three To Get Ready* is not a rehash of material readily available elsewhere. The book is original in concept. John G. Quesnell has sifted through his own experience, both as a married man and as a marriage and family counselor, to bring fresh insight to a variety of issues relative today to engaged couples.

Because of his bias, the author speaks about marriage very positively, but he maintains a candid realism. Not only does he talk about the "warm fuzzies" of engagement and marriage but he also discusses the "cold pricklies" and how to best deal with them. In reading the book, you soon get the impression — "Hey! This fellow knows what he's talking about! He's got something to tell me!"

John Quesnell possesses a good deal of knowledge, experience, and skill with marital questions, but he is not an "expert" who has "got it made" speaking to us from "on high." Strikingly evident is that he himself has grown and developed in his ideas and attitudes concerning marriage. In this he has obviously received help and support from his wife Alice.

Not only does the author speak with knowledge but he also speaks in practical down-to-earth terms. He has enlightened his narrative with a blend of concrete examples and amusing and pertinent stories. Thus the reader does not get mired in a bog of terminology and verbosity. The book is enjoyable to read.

Some readers may glance through the chapters and say, "Well, this looks like a fine book, but once we're married it won't be of any use to us, so we may as well not buy it just for the short period of our engagement."

Actually, one of the fine points about *Three To Get Ready* is that it doesn't become outdated when the engagement period is over and the couple is married. It can be used and referred to again and again during a marriage.

The book is not meant to be read by each partner on one, two, or even three sittings and then put aside. It's meant to provoke thought and initiate discussion between them on the vital issues of their marriage.

In discussing these issues each person will have to look inside himself, listen to his partner, and be open to looking at life and marriage in a Christian way.

All in all, whoever reads *Three To Get Ready* will have a profitable experience. Engaged couples will certainly find the material valuable for their own relationship.

A. J. (Reb) Materi, O.M.I.

INTRODUCTION

As a result of my work as a marriage and family counselor and educator, it has become glaringly evident to me that there is a dramatic difference between Christian and secular marriage. The title *Three To Get Ready* introduces the reader to the central meaning of Christian engagement and marriage. That union will only exist when they vow to become husband and wife. Engagement is a *betrothal* of man and woman to each other and marriage is a *union* of man and woman. Most engaged couples do not have an opportunity to be exposed to and develop an understanding of the meaning of Christian engagement and marriage. Our media and the courses conducted in most high schools and colleges focus so totally upon secular marriage that a couple runs the risk of either thinking there is only one style of marriage or actually believing that secular and Christian engagement and marriage are synonymous.

During the past several years my wife Alice and I have worked with thousands of couples preparing for marriage. Our initial experiences caused us to look cynically upon this apostolate. The attitude of the couples suggested, "We love each other, that's all that is needed for marriage, and there is no one who can tell us anything we don't already know." Because of this attitude we were tempted to focus more upon marriage enrichment programs as after a few years of marriage couples are more open to exploring various ways to enhance the marital relationship. Because of this greater openness it was easier to be involved in an apostolate with the married. Fortunately, over the years our attitude changed. A modification of content and technique created a greater receptivity by the engaged. Also, we began to understand how much the engaged could profit from a program specifically geared to their needs.

We look upon engagement and marriage as a time of critical transition in one's life, a point having the potential for dramatic change and a point from which there is no turning back. One's life will never again be the same.

As we began to recognize the critical nature of engagement, we realized an educational program for the engaged could have one of two thrusts. One could develop a program designed to say nicey-nice things in a nicey-nice way. Theoretically, the engaged would develop nicey-nice feelings and leave such a program feeling warm fuzzies toward each other as well as the instructors, or a program for the engaged potentially could truly help couples turn around their lives. We recognized that the tumultuous 1960s had created an environment which prompted many young people to stray from practicing their faith. We realized that a positive experience with the structure and representatives of the institutional Church could prompt couples to re-explore the possibility of once again participating in their Church and bringing themselves into a closer union with our Lord. We opted to be involved in programs offering couples this opportunity.

Christian marriage means living the challenges of marriage with Christian dedication. The secular challenges of marriage revolve around communication, finances, and sex. For the Christian couple the challenges revolve around understanding equality, decision making, and authority; coming to grips with love and sexuality; and understanding the nature and meaning of a spiritual relationship.

Although *Three To Get Ready* is written by a Catholic and is based upon the philosophy and theology of that religion, hopefully the faithful of other denominations will find the suggested ideas helpful. I am especially hopeful that those who have strayed away from the protective love of our Lord and Savior will again be stirred to bring themselves under the umbrella of his protection.

I have not intended to duplicate what the reader could easily find in available materials. Neither have I intended to write about what other authors more competently have covered. For this reason suggested readings are listed at the end of each section. For the interested engaged couple or pastor, these references will provide a more in-depth treatment of specific areas.

It is Alice's and my prayer that *Three to Get Ready* will help the reader come to a deeper understanding of himself, the significant other, and Christian engagement and marriage. We have prayed that the practical suggestions will help a couple deal with the nitty-gritty tasks of engagement and marriage. Most importantly, we pray that the reader will truly become interested in walking more closely with our Lord. It is that kind of walk that can radically turn about one's life.

John G. Quesnell

SECTION I

ENGAGEMENT:
A TIME FOR KNOWING
ME, YOU, AND GOD

1

LOVE IS PATIENT AND KIND

Congratulations to the engaged couples who have witnessed to their love and faith in each other by solemnly promising to marry. In making this promise, a conscientious couple must prepare not only for the wedding day but also for married life. Preparation for the wedding involves both preparation for a ceremony and an interior preparation of the self. Preparation for marriage asks that one be brave enough to look seriously at *oneself*, as well as the *relationship* into which he has promised to enter.

Considering the attitude of the larger society toward marriage, it is all the more important to congratulate an engaged couple. The Christian community must do all that is possible to support a couple's decision by helping them prepare for their wedding and marriage.

Would you ask yourself if our society takes marriage seriously or even if it approves of marriage? What was the reaction of friends, relatives, and the larger community to your engagement? Once, while in a barber shop, I heard a man in his early twenties announce that he would be married the next evening. The men in the shop began the usual litany of, "Sucker," "If I had my life to live over again...," "Misery loves company," etc. The young man's face dropped and he exclaimed, "That makes one thousand and six. Isn't anyone happily married?" For a marriage counselor sitting with six unhappily married men, this was a tremendous opportunity for group therapy! When I asked whether it was true that everyone was so unhappily married, the men admitted their happiness and replied, "A good wife is the best gift one can have," "Welcome aboard," etc. Most men have been so influenced by the pseudo-masculine world that they do not realize it is permissible to speak positively about marriage. As the men talked further, the young man's face brightened and he exclaimed, "I'm happy to hear that some people are happily married."

Consider other examples of what marriage means to some people. A week prior to his wedding, one man's fellow railroad employees locked him in a boxcar and shipped him off to another state to spare him the fate of marriage. Another man was skiing with friends in Colorado just prior to his wedding. As they sat in one of the local watering holes, his friends commented, "Tom, why do you want to get married? You are a successful engineer and a happy bachelor. You have life made! Why bother marrying?" Not wanting to become party to this negative thinking, Tom exclaimed, "So I don't have to spend the rest of my life with guys like you in places like this!"

The women's liberation emphasis today has meant that women also react negatively to marriage. Many fiancées explain that after announcing their engagement to friends at work they have received one or two sympathy cards. Some will comment that these friends were only kidding and such remarks should not be taken seriously. However, these remarks condition one to think negatively about the state of marriage and interfere with one's freedom to fully celebrate the sacrament.

Although it is an extremely sensitive issue, I ask you to consider that the bachelor party can be a pagan practice which compromises one's freedom to celebrate marriage. In some instances this same criticism can be made of bridal showers. Two mental attitudes are associated with the bachelor party. The first recognizes that a marriage is a significant event in one's life to which many friends celebrate. For these people the bachelor party is an opportunity to get together with old friends.

I take exception with the second mental attitude which is based on the premise, "Poor old Dick is biting the dust, the ball and chain will be locked on him, and we've got to take him out and hang on a good one before he is out of circulation." Once, after discussing sexuality with some engaged couples and explaining that no eleventh commandment says, "Thou must have intercourse the first day of marriage," a man exclaimed, "Well, Jack, I'm sure glad to hear that. All my buddies will be at the wedding and we will be so drunk I won't be able to find the bed!"

This negative attitude toward marriage is also exemplified by comments such as, "Whether you marry or not, you will live to regret it"; "Marriage is the only institution in which the hunted pays for the license"; and "Married men live longer than single men, so if you want to die a slow death, get married." This attitude carries into marriage, so that spouses (like the men in the barber shop) need special permission to be positive about their marriage and treat their wives with loving respect and kindness. Thus, if a man is asked to stop with some guys after work, he says, "I'd like to go with you guys, but I was late getting home a month ago and I haven't heard the end of it yet!" This negative comment is acceptable to our society, but it would be unacceptable to say, "I'd like to go with you guys, but Sue and I have not had much opportunity to be together this week. We are both going to be home tonight and I really want to be with her." The difference between these two explanations may be subtle, but the tendency to respond in the negative has an erosive effect upon the marriage.

The negative outlook toward marriage is reflected by the attitude many men have toward planning the wedding.

The groom may say, "I don't want anything to do with the planning. That's a woman's job. Just keep it as simple as possible so we can get out of there!" This unfortunate attitude detracts from the true celebration of the wedding.

On top of not having societal permission to celebrate marriage, Christians and Jews must wonder if they believe marriage symbolizes God's covenant with his people. Catholics must also wonder whether they truly believe marriage is a sacrament. There is a double standard applied to the Catholic sacraments of holy orders and matrimony. For instance, if one has a brother or sister being ordained a priest or professing final vows in religious life, everyone would be shocked if they heard about a drunken party the night before. There would be calls to the local pastor, if not to the bishop. How different it is for marriage when "hanging one on" seems to be the norm.

With this in mind consider these three types of church weddings. In the "convenience" church wedding the couple asks that their marriage be witnessed by an ordained minister to please their parents or because it hasn't occurred to them that a civil marriage might be less expensive. The couple feels no real commitment to the sacramental meaning of marriage and little desire to enter into a truly spiritual relationship.

In the "nicey-nice" church wedding each party wants to have their marriage witnessed by an ordained minister of the Lord, but they are not actually aware of the power of this sacrament or covenant. They appreciate the nice altar with its flowers, the acoustics of the building, and the aisle down which they can walk. Beyond that, there is little appreciation for the truly sacramental meaning of marriage.

In the truly sacramental marriage the couple is aware of the power of this sacrament and covenant and look at the church wedding as an opportunity to go to the home of their Father to ask his blessing upon their union. In discussing marriage as a sacrament and covenant, a couple should realize that a covenant differs radically from a contract. A covenant is an unbreakable agreement epitomized by the covenant between God and Israel. In spite of the failure of Israel to remain faithful to Yahweh, he remained true to them. God uses the story of Hosea and Gomer to reveal his own fidelity to his people. This story stands in such radical opposition to contemporary standards that modern couples have trouble relating to it. Hosea, in spite of Gomer's unfaithfulness, remains faithful to her. He is willing to forgive, though he is humiliated in the betrayal. He did this because his marriage was a covenant (not only a contract which is kept as long as the other party also follows the terms) to which God expected him to remain faithful.

Whereas a contract limits and narrows, a covenant marriage is a partnership of life and love in which there is no "mine" and "thine" and in which the expectations are total. A covenant marriage has God as author, witness, and guarantor. Fr. Paul Palmer points out that of the many words the Romans used for marriage, they preferred *foedus*, covenant. The root meaning of the word is to trust another and to entrust oneself wholly to the other. Built into the word is the idea of fidelity (*fides*).[1]

When Christ established his Church, Christians began to look upon marriage as a sacrament. While most Protestant traditions recognize baptism and the Eucharist as sacraments, the Catholic Church recognizes marriage as one of seven sacraments. This does not imply that Protestant Churches place any less importance on marriage. It is viewed as a sacred reality because it reflects and symbolizes the marriage (or love) of Christ with his Church. Since it is based upon and is to reflect the love of Christ for his Church, marriage is a supernatural event where the mutual love expressed is a participation in the love Christ has for his Church.

---

[1] Paul Palmer, "Shall We Make a Covenant?", *The Priest*, (July-August, 1975), p. 15.

The Catholic Church views marriage as a symbol of Christ's covenant with his Church and a participation in that covenant. Through the grace of Christ natural love is perfected, the indissoluble unity is strengthened, and the spouses are sanctified (Council of Trent). A sacrament is the visible and historical manifestation of God to man. This also implies that the sacrament includes a special grace from God, giving us the power (if we want it) to fulfill our mission. Since it symbolizes the redemption and love which Christ brings to his Church, Christian marriage is a miniature church wherein husband and wife live and sacrifice for each other out of love. Husband and wife are called upon to be to each other what Christ is to each of us. When a marriage is in the Lord, every expression of caring becomes a source of grace.

Couples should discuss the three types of marriage, identify the kind they plan to enter, and discuss the meaning of a covenant marriage. At the age of marriage many people experience a feeling of rebellion against the Church or simply indifference toward it. The wedding can be an opportunity to reassess one's relationship with God and rebuild this relationship. There may have also been some unhappy experiences with the institutional Church. Perhaps the wedding can provide a couple with an opportunity to restabilize their relationship with the Church which God has provided to speak to us. Many couples find it helpful to work with the clergyman who will witness their wedding, to talk with him not only about plans for the wedding but also for assistance in preparing themselves. Perhaps through this relationship a couple will become sufficiently open to God's word that they will want a truly sacramental marriage.

If, however, a couple only desires a "convenience" type church wedding, they should question whether or not they are compromising the Church and its minister by going through the motions of a church ceremony. There is a distinction between a legal marriage and the sacrament of matrimony.

The couple who is open to a Christian marriage may want to consider solemnizing their engagement, a ceremony witnessed by a clergyman – often the one who will witness the wedding – and along with the promise to marry is a request that Jesus be a part of the engagement. In essence, a couple would promise to live their engagement in a way consistent with Jesus' teachings, seeking to understand whether it is his will that they marry. The solemnization underscores engagement as a time of mental and spiritual preparation for marriage. It is not an irrevocable promise, as is marriage itself. It is a promise to treat each other with the utmost respect and to marry if each continues to desire marriage to each other and if the engagement suggests sufficient compatibility, ability to resolve differences, and deep enough love. It is a sign of their willingness to let the Spirit guide their decision to marry. Solemnization recognizes that the couple has supernatural as well as natural powers available to them to meet the challenges associated with making that decision to marry and preparing themselves for marriage.

It is my prayer that couples will desire a sacramental wedding and Christian marriage. One thrust of this book is to encourage couples to develop the kind of spiritual relationship which will cause them to substitute an evening of prayer for the bachelor party. Because of the seriousness of their relationship with Christ, hopefully one or two weeks before their wedding couples will want to invite their very close friends and family to gather for a special evening of prayer to spiritually prepare the people for the wedding day and ask for the Lord's blessing on that glorious day.

2

LOVE IS NOT ILL-MANNERED

A natural extension of the earlier suggestion that society does not grant permission to celebrate marriage is the additional notion that many do not take their marriages seriously.

We recall the magical idea that one marries to live happily ever after, settle down, and raise a family. Rather than marry and settle down, many people marry and "settle in." That is, they settle into an old age or senescence of marriage.

Couples seem to settle into a kind of marriage in which they neglect some of what made courtship dynamic and exciting. Consider the husband who has gained fifteen pounds during the first year of marriage. He sits around the house in his favorite outfit — jockey shorts and a t-shirt with a hole in the belly for better ventilation. If a friend calls asking if he is busy, he replies, "No, not doing anything at all. I'm here by myself, just sitting around with my wife." Suddenly his wife is equated with being nobody.

Unfortunately, his wife may not do much better. She is running around the house in her favorite outfit — cut-offs, an old sweatshirt, and hair wrapped up in beer cans (her contribution to ecology.) If a friend phones, she replies that neither is she doing anything, no one is there, and she's just sitting around the house with her husband.

If one were to stand on a busy street corner and watch couples drive by, he could predict whether they were going together, engaged, or married just by where each sat in the car. An older married couple (married about three years) may drive past a church. The wife may become somewhat nostalgic and comment, "Remember when we were married?" Then she glances at the chasm between them and comments, "My, how far apart we've grown in these three years of marriage." In typical male fashion the husband may respond, "Well, Sue, I haven't moved." Rather than placing a premium upon not moving, married couples need to focus upon growing together and learning to appreciate the depth of love available to them.

It is not only married couples who run the risk of falling into senescence. The engaged are equally likely to fall into this trap. It is the wise couple who examines their relationship to identify symptoms of the "old age of engagement."

One of the common traps into which engaged couples fall is becoming more tuned in to TV than to each other. They generally rationalize this by explaining that TV is the only thing they can afford. It gives them an opportunity to be together without having to spend money they do not have. Unfortunately, this is a convenient cop-out as most couples discover that TV is like a third person coming between them. One partner may begin to say something only to be interrupted with, "Shhh, I'm into this program. Let's talk about it later." At the commercial that partner may turn to the other asking, "What did you want?" The other partner will then be wrapped up in the commercial. Before long they have forgotten what it was they wanted to say to each other.

We have noticed a certain verbal impoverishment among many engaged couples. Is it because they become so wrapped up in watching TV that they do not learn to talk to each other? Another risk of the engaged is that they may learn to communicate only in braille and not try to become acquainted with the other's total person. Some suggest that the amount of enjoyment gained from an activity is directly related to the energy exerted. Couples should consider energy-exerting activities as tennis, softball, swimming, or hiking. There are several admission-free activities that are much more active and helpful than TV to a couple who is seeking to build their relationship.

Frequently, the simple ability to be nice to each other is one of the dimensions missing in the engaged relationship. It is distressing to overhear the abusive way in which some engaged couples talk to each other. Engagement does not give license to overlook the common courtesies of life.

Immediately after our wedding Alice and I and our families greeted our guests in the back of the church. My father-in-law turned to me, shook my hand, and said, "Jack, be nice to each other." Since I had just graduated from college the week before, I doubted that a man at age fifty-five would have anything relevant to say to me about marriage. So, it wasn't until some years later that I recalled that practical advice from a very nice man. We ask that engaged couples consider the impact of that very simple statement and ask themselves if they are, indeed, being nice to each other. They might be reminded that best friends laugh and talk together and treat each other with kindness, courtesy, and respect. Couples should ask themselves if they bother to say three nice things to each other each time they are together.

As the wedding day approaches some engaged couples become concerned that they have fallen out of love. Many notice that they do not feel as excited toward each other as they did when they began going together. Most certainly, this is something to take seriously. However, before a couple concludes that it has fallen out of love, it is wise to consider that they may have evolved from a romantic love to a more mature love which prepares them for marriage. Romantic love is that feeling of bells ringing and a blast furnace burning at the base of one's heart. However, mature love simmers down to a temperature which is tolerable in both summer and winter. One man, considering engagement, explained, "It must be love! Every time I see her, my heart pounds like a trip hammer." It could be love, but it may have been a mild "heart attack." Mature love recognizes that love does not spring willy-nilly from good intentions alone as Minerva sprang from the head of Zeus. Human love in all its forms requires painstaking cultivation, concentration, and pursuit of knowledge of the self and the other. Speaking against romantic love, George Bernard Shaw explained, "People in love are under the influence of the most violent, most insane, most elusive, and most transient of passions and they are required to swear that they will remain in that excited, abnormal, and exhausting condition until death do them part."

This discussion may cause some wonder about prenuptial jitters, a term which describes the last minute doubts some couples have about marriage. Couples may require more understanding of this than the simple comment, "Everyone goes through this. You will be OK after the wedding."

If a fiancé or fiancée generally panics over most anything – examinations, driving in traffic, a new job, etc. – he or she need not be alarmed by pre-nuptial jitters. Such reaction is normal to a stress situation. But, if it is out of all proportion to the usual, it would be well to seriously consider this "gut-level reaction." It may be a message that the party has some very serious question about going through with the marriage. The meaning of this reaction should be thoroughly explored before, rather than after, the marriage. It should never be summarily disregarded.

Essentially, couples should remember that the feeling of falling out of love may actually be mature love substituted for romantic love. Couples must form a mental attitude which continually involves them in developing their love relationship. They might consider that love is like a rose garden. If the garden is neglected, the roses will be overgrown by weeds. If love is not nurtured, it will suffocate.

3

THE COLD PRICKLIES

Although *Three to Get Ready* is very positive and optimistic about marriage, it would be unfair to not discuss how couples can constructively deal with differences. After touching on the "warm fuzzies" of engagement, one should deal with some "cold pricklies." In seminars and retreats for the engaged, we always feel very badly if a couple objects to a discussion of differences, explaining, "There is no need to talk about disagreements. If we had any, we would not be marrying." It may be true that some very compatible and placid people do not have disagreements. However, as a result of our individual differences and the talents God has given us, most partners view matters in different ways. In most instances, if a couple has no disagreements, one of them is unnecessary.

As a couple reads this, it would be helpful to discuss how to deal with their differences. Basically, a couple should develop the mental attitude of working out, rather than fighting out, problems. The statement, "Fighting is better than being bored. You might get killed, but at least you know you're alive while it's going on," depicts how very damaging a competitive relationship can become.

It is helpful for engaged couples to ask themselves how they express their disagreements, "The tune makes the music." How one says something affects the eventual resolution. One wife, who always accentuated the positive, was confronted by her angry husband, "I don't want to hear any bad news, just give me the good news." She responded, "Well, three of our four children did not break an arm today." If a couple cannot talk about their differences, senseless little islands of secrecy develop which eat away at the relationship. Being aware of the normalcy of differences, Christian couples ought then to learn to deal with them in a loving and charitable way.

For instance, a fiancée may recognize an imperfection in her husband-to be, as did one woman who discovered that her future mother-in-law thought her son was absolutely perfect. When they announced their engagement, the mother-in-law-to-be hugged her son's fiancée exclaiming, "You are a lucky girl. Richard has been a most satisfactory son." With that, the fiancée glanced up to the mantle where she saw a colored picture of her fiancé illuminated by a vigil candle. Apparently, the mother believed in perpetual adoration.

One has to face the reality of imperfections. As a result of these imperfections, one's partner may find it necessary to criticize or offer little suggestions for improvement. Couples must ask themselves if they have learned to offer constructive criticism. Criticism, like rain, should be gentle enough to nourish man's growth without destroying his roots. Couples must also ask themselves how they receive criticism. "Do I tend to be a Defensive Denny or Denise who denies all faults?"

Couples might consider the "HALT" approach to constructively deal with differences. This approach recognizes that at certain times our mood and temperament demand that the best thing we can do is drop the whole subject, agreeing to pick it up later. Each letter represents a particular mood that generally interferes with the resolution of differences:

H — Hungry
A — Angry
L — Lonely
T — Tired

"H" suggests that some of us find it best not to discuss certain problems on an empty stomach. After eating we may be in a much more conciliatory frame of mind.

For "A," please ask yourselves whether you have ever been angry at each other. If you have, ask yourself if when you were angry you ever said something you did not mean. If the answer to this is also yes, take the next step and ask if you knew at the very moment you were saying it that you did not mean it. Many of us become angry at our partner, say things we don't mean, and realize at that very moment that we don't mean it. It is as though we just can't control ourselves — "the devil made me do it!" At these times we should realize that we are too angry to be constructive and we should talk about it later. It is unfortunate that even if we apologize immediately, explaining, "I didn't mean it," an unnecessary hurt remains in the heart of the other. Of course, these things must be forgiven.

If a couple has been separated from each other for a while, it is best to give each other the TLC (tender loving care) each needs before discussing sensitive issues.

Some people find it ill-advised to discuss sensitive issues when they are tired. Although Scripture suggests that man should not let the sun set upon his anger, some of us fear that if we do not let the sun set upon our anger, we will be up all night fighting. Some people find they become terribly sensitive, paranoid, and "bleed" very easily when fatigued. For instance, I returned late one Sunday evening from a busy weekend retreat. I had looked forward to relaxing and talking with Alice. Unfortunately, we made the mistake of talking about a very sensitive issue — we were doing some remodeling in the house and we began talking about where the materials should be stored. No doubt all readers have experienced "deep gut-level hurt." Certainly, to have your suggestion rejected regarding the storage of building materials is the "deepest hurt" one can imagine. Fortunately, as the discussion became heated, Alice had the presence of mind to exclaim, "HALT!" We were too tired and lonely to discuss something so "sensitive and important." Some eight hours later neither of us really cared where the materials were piled. On the previous evening we each needed TLC and not a discussion about remodeling.

Other than the feelings that are created when one is hungry, angry, lonely, or tired, at times a person will be in a down mood that the other should respect. Men and women experience various emotions as a result of circadian cycles which cause a constant 24-hour rhythmic flux of hormones, moods, strengths, and weaknesses. As we sleep and wake our body temperature rises and falls with our hormones, and this causes a rise and fall of efficiency and libido. Our moods affect the efficiency with which we can approach marital discord.

People often seem more aware of the mood of the wife, as it is closely tied to her menstrual cycle. One of the several advantages of Natural Family Planning, discussed in Section III, is that a couple becomes more attuned to the effect physical changes have upon a woman's emotional life. It is said that a man who is unaware of his fiancée's menstrual cycle deserves what he gets. The sensitive man recognizes that at certain times each month letting some things drop is showing love. It is best to let some issues remain unchallenged. He may notice there is little he can do right. Rather than letting his pride cause him to feel he must object to her behavior and defend his, the understanding fiancé seeks to comfort and console. The effects of premenstrual tension caused one husband to quip,

"There ought to be pills for husbands to take during this time."

It is the chauvinist who contends, "It's all in her head." Premenstrual tension is a result of generalized fluid retention, some of which causes a swelling in the cerebral area, resulting in headaches. The severity of a woman's premenstrual tension varies from cycle to cycle, and this is accompanied by some physiological change. A woman notices hyperirritability, headaches, nervousness, bloating, weight gain, and fluid retention. These conditions are caused by ovarian hormones late in the menstrual cycle.

In summary, the loving couple should accept interpersonal differences. They should realize that their own perspective is subjective and that a particular problem or difference of opinion may have several acceptable solutions. They should not see their disagreements as fights but rather as opportunities to develop a deeper awareness of and appreciation for each other. They should understand that disagreements are creative only if each learns something new about the other, if they provide growth opportunities, and if the couple arrives at mutual decisions that are more satisfactory than if each had acted singly.

4

LOVE DOES NOT KEEP
A RECORD OF WRONGS

The humble couple looks at some of the undesirable ways in which they deal with their differences. As one considers the things he does to interfere with resolving differences, he begins to see how personal pride hinders him. When we become wrapped up in our prideful defenses, it is very difficult to constructively resolve differences which arise daily.

For instance, consider Peaceful Percy who wants absolutely no hassle. Percy walks about with a gunnysack, stuffing all his problems into it, proudly proclaiming, "Nothing bothers me." Percy shouts, "I don't get mad very often, but when I do, watch out!" or "I don't get mad very often, but when I do, it takes me a long time to get over it." In reality, Percy is puffed up with pride and his distorted sense of masculinity causes him to believe that men are always calm, cool, collected, and unaffected by trauma. He fancies himself as the strong silent type who sits very tall in the saddle.

One Peaceful Percy was engaged to a woman, expert at acupuncture. While she needled him, Percy calmly explained that nothing bothered him. When I suggested that some of her remarks were below the belt, he simply explained, "Jack, you're far too sensitive, these things don't bother me a bit." However, after marriage, we discovered Percy did not forget a thing. He took the needling for several months and then went out and really "hung one on." He returned home early in the morning, got his wife out of bed, set her down at the table, pulled out each needle, dipped it in a cup of poison, and zinged it right back at her. It would have been much better if Percy had taken hold of his pride and talked about the things that hurt him.

Another couple returned for an appointment after a village election in which the wife had run for an office. When I asked about the outcome of the election, she explained, "I lost, but overall it was a very good experience and I'm glad I did it." When I asked the husband how he had reacted to the campaign, he said, "I didn't like it at all." His surprised wife asked, "Why didn't you tell me? I thought you approved and I don't understand why you're saying you didn't like it." The husband explained that he thought it would have been useless to say anything to his wife. Not knowing when to keep my mouth shut, I then asked how he voted. He had voted for the other candidate, and his wife lost the election by one vote!

A Percy is an extremely difficult person to live with because it may take several years to discover he has been hurt. It may take six months, a year, five years, or twenty years, but inevitably it will come out. Another Percy scheduled an appointment for him and his wife but explained nothing to her. This champion gunnysacker explained, "We have been married for twenty-two years, we've never had a fight, but I want a divorce." His shocked wife could not understand what was happening and asked, "I don't understand, what's wrong, why do you want a divorce?" Percy explained, "You don't love me!" Then he told why he thought his wife didn't love him and opened his gunnysack and brought out what had caused hurt during their twenty-two years of marriage and one year courtship. His wife, as do the wives of all Percys, sat in a shocked state, repeating, "I never knew that hurt you. Why didn't you tell me?" Poor old Percy thought that if his wife really loved him, she would not do anything he didn't like. So, without even the benefit of a crystal ball for a wedding present, Percy expected his wife to be aware of his emotional needs, likes and dislikes, and expectations of marriage. Unfortunately, he never bothered to tell her about any of those needs, sensitive spots, or expectations. It seems that he wanted so badly to avoid an argument that he started a fight. Couples are involved in a continual process of adjusting to each other's differences. The mind becomes boggled if one considers the prospect of trying to adjust in a marriage in which one partner refuses to talk about differences and yet interprets each difference as a sign that he is not loved.

Silent Sal is very much like Percy. When something is amiss, she turns on the loud silence. She refuses to reply when her fiancé asks, "What's wrong?" When he persists, explaining, "We will never be able to resolve anything if you won't tell me what is the matter." She turns her head, complaining, "It hurts too much to talk about it." When he persists further, she asks, "You really don't know?" If he persists further, she may exclaim, "If you don't know, you really are a sickey!" Like Percy, pride has a stranglehold on Sal and she seems unable to help her partner resolve their impasse.

Couples can generally operate upon the premise that expressed anger goes away and suppressed anger comes out elsewhere. Sarcasm is one of the very destructive ways in which suppressed anger comes out. Sarcasm is a "neat little trick." If one partner reacts to the sarcasm, the other can respond, "My, aren't we sensitive! Can't you even take a little joke?" If the sarcasm brings no response, the sarcastic one can later say, "Well, I told you about it and you didn't care enough to understand what I was saying." Sarcasm is a passive-aggressive way, which society seemingly approves, of dealing with feelings. "Knock your partner" is one of the more popular parlor games played by couples. As the knocking goes back and forth, others may think, "Don't Tom and Jane have fun? Look how they kid each other." To understand that it is not kidding, one would have to see what happens with Tom and Jane when they leave the others.

One woman explained her concern when some good friends seemed to continually give excuses for not getting together. Finally, she asked the woman if there had been a misunderstanding or if something had happened. The woman explained, "It has nothing to do with you, Julie; it's just that whenever we get together, Dick is so sarcastic and mean to me." As it turned out, Julie explained that it was the same with her husband. As they talked about it, they discovered that each husband thought the sarcasm of the other was "cute." So, when they got together they competed to see who could be more sarcastic toward his wife. The hurt of each wife was ample proof that nothing was funny. Fortunately, they straightened this out and the husbands came to understand the meaning of their sarcasm.

For most couples disagreements and hurts are inevitable. Also, in spite of our best resolutions, our actions may get us into a deeper mire. So, it is necessary to examine how to deal with differences and make a conscious effort to change those ways which are destructive to the relationship. However, recognizing that a couple may yet do things which hurt the other, each should examine his or her attitude toward asking for and granting forgiveness. Again, there is a dramatic difference between Christian and secular marriage. The secularist may believe that "love is never having to say you're sorry." The Christian, however, recognizes the importance of apologizing and asking for forgiveness. Many are familiar with the idea that "half the fun of having a fight is making up." This implies that after asking for and receiving forgiveness a couple discovers a reassuring sense of closeness. One has to wonder if the grace of our Lord enters very specially into the lives of those who are willing to live life as he taught. It is perhaps this grace that enables a forgiving couple to discover a deeper sense of union. As an imperfect human being, I know I will do things that will hurt my wife and children. When that happens I must pray for the grace to conquer my pride and ask for forgiveness. Yet, there are times that I so badly want to grant my wife forgiveness or say I'm sorry but find it hard to get hold of the pride and drop that which has upset us.

Frequently, couples hassle about who is to apologize first. An example from the Air Force is helpful here. During a three-week orientation recruits were asked, "When officers of equal rank meet, who initiates the salute?" The correct response was, "The gentleman salutes first." This applies to marriage in that the gentle person apologizes and makes it possible for the couple to be reconciled.

It is as difficult, if not more so, to grant forgiveness as it is to ask for it. We may have an attitude of, "You have hurt me, your sorries don't count, and you're going to have to suffer a good deal longer before I'll be willing to talk with you." Couples must remember that "he who cannot forgive others destroys the bridge over which he himself must pass."

Hopefully, the Christian couple will develop a prayer life into which is integrated an assessment of their response to the gospel and to the expectations of Christian marriage. In essence, one is asking, "Where am I in relationship to my faith and others?" This assessment will remind couples of ways in which they have hurt the other and will give them the opportunity to ask the other for forgiveness and to turn to our Lord and ask his forgiveness. In a very real sense spouses are ordained to a ministry of healing. We are called to minister to each other's needs and hurts — especially to the hurts we have caused.

5

MY WAY IS MY WAY

In response to a study suggesting that a woman often marries a man similar to her father, a woman responded, "I guess that's why mothers cry at weddings." Despite its facetious tone, this suggests that spouses from similar backgrounds tend to be happier in marriage. It seems that, in spite of any fantasy we may have of ourselves as adaptable and adjustable, we have an easier time being married to someone who has likes, dislikes, interests, and viewpoints similar to ours. For this reason it is important for engaged couples to talk about their own family life, the life-style to which they were exposed, and contrast the similarities and dissimilarities. Another person quipped, "If you wonder what your wife is going to look like in twenty years, look at her mother. It may not be that mother and daughter will look alike, but they certainly may act and think alike.

When couples marry they are often involved in the process of emancipating themselves from their parents, establishing their own identity, and perhaps even rebelling against the life-style, codes, and mores of their parents. Yet, there is much to suggest that by their mid to late twenties, a person's interests and outlooks are more similar than dissimilar to his parents. To the extent that this is true, it is helpful for the engaged to spend time with each other's family to examine how well they get along. There is some truth to the idea that the ability to get along with the other's family suggests something about their own ability to get along. This concept holds especially true for those who have a happy relationship with their parents. If one has had good family experiences, he tends to want to live in a similar way in order to recreate that good experience in his marriage.

If one has had unhappy family experiences, the task is somewhat more difficult. Those coming from unhappy families may know what they do not want instead of knowing what they do want. This is like shopping for a gift when one is only aware of what he doesn't want to purchase. Those who have had unhappy family experiences should talk about what they want their marriage to be like rather than what they don't want it to be like. They should seek a positive model and identify with it.

We also encourage couples to discuss the possibility of seeking parental approval of their marriage. This may sound old-fashioned, but it is a courtesy and the couple may profit from their parents' reaction and advice. Most parents have a never-ending interest in their children and want them to be happily married. Many parents also have a penetrating awareness of their children and an uncanny ability to identify whether or not an anticipated marriage is wise. In our work with engaged couples, we have found that most of them have never considered asking parental permission. However, as they thought about it, they saw wisdom in it, decided to backtrack, and reported that they learned a good deal from their parents' response and a very favorable bond was created between them and their parents.

I spent several years pouting because Alice's parents did not seem overjoyed about taking me into their family. As indicated earlier they would not have responded as emotionally to anything as I would have liked, but I did wonder if they approved of our marriage. Although I expected them to welcome me with open arms, it never occurred to me that I should ask their permission to marry. Some years after our marriage I realized how discourteous this was and asked my father-in-law if it had hurt him. He explained that it had been painful and perhaps it was something I would better understand as our children grew older. As he talked about his own commitment to his family, I realized how hard it must have been for him to accept our marrying just after I had graduated from college and just before I entered graduate school. It was totally alien to his values that any man should marry when he did not even have a job.

If the parents approve of the marriage, they may have some helpful observations regarding the positive and negative features of the relationship. The mature couple can then take these comments seriously and profit from them. After the parents have given approval, a couple may want to ask for a parental blessing upon the engagement. Perhaps this can occur as part of the solemnization ceremony.

However, what does a couple do if the parents disapprove of the engagement? Most certainly, the objections must be taken seriously. If the couple accepts the objections, they first should explore the possibility of making the changes suggested by the objection. This may only amount to delaying marriage until one has found employment. It may mean some personality change by one partner or the other, or it may call for a more effective adjustment to differences in life-style.

Some parents may either grant or deny permission because of one of their problems. Some parents may indiscreetly approve of a marriage to get a "child" off their hands, to straighten out a son or daughter with whom they have been having difficulty, or to solve some other problem. Others may indiscreetly disapprove because it is hard for them to see their children leave home, because they believe no one is good enough for their son or daughter, or because of a more complicated psychological problem.

Couples should understand that the motivation for the parental response must also be understood. Thus, the response need not necessarily be taken carte blanche. But, please consider that engaged couples are often too quick to discount parental opinions.

Considering all the jokes about in-laws, most couples come to appreciate and love their in-laws. The engaged couple should appreciate that parents have some ambivalent feelings as they watch their sons and daughters emancipate themselves. It is not easy to see a loved one leave them and cling to another. Both the parents and the engaged need to strive for greater understanding.

A common source of tension revolves around the question, "Whose wedding is it — the parents' or the engaged couple's?" Although the parents need to appreciate that they had their day, the couple should consider their parents' wishes regarding the style of the wedding, its site, and the guest list. No wedding should put anyone in the poor house.

A very special tension is created for the interfaith couple when one or both families object to "the other religion." The next chapter comments on this and suggests how to cope with these special problems. In planning a wedding families may have ample opportunity to practice the HALT approach.

Essentially, the engaged have spent several years learning a particular family's life-style. Entering marriage is like entering a neutral, but foreign, country where one must learn a new language. Even if each partner comes from very similar backgrounds, it will no longer be acceptable to do things in their own individual way. They must develop a couple, rather than individual, identity.

Because of our own cultural backgrounds, Alice and I learned that entering marriage was something like a guy from France and a gal from Germany being dropped into a neutral country. During the first five or six years of our marriage, we experienced an ill-defined tension. One day, as we were approaching Alice's folks' home, our daughter commented, "Let me see, we're going to Grandma and Grandpa Lehar's. They will shake my hand. It's Grandma and Grandpa Quesnell who kiss me." With that, Alice and I could only comment, "Out of the mouths of babes...." We looked at each other realizing that Cathy had identified the source of tension we had experienced.

I looked upon Alice's family as being austere Germans who probably didn't like me. On the other hand Alice looked upon my family as a group of hysterics. She could never understand why we hugged and kissed each other when we met and why my dad got out a bath towel so everybody could cry when we left. Alice thought we were going to see each other again and there was no reason for all the fuss. As the years go by we continue to see that these French and German patterns are deeply ingrained and that married love requires a continual adjustment to these differences.

When couples are inclined to waste time trying to prove one style better than the other, they should recall the Irish adage, "He who tills the soil becomes a slave to it." Is this better than the German idea that God has given us the soil as a gift and we are required to care for it? Depending upon one's perspective, each may be right.

Learning a new language has proven very real to us. After spending several years in a mobile home, we decided to be like many other Americans who were saddled with house payments. After my father-in-law approved of the house we planned to buy, he explained, "We know that you and Alice have worked hard for this house and we want to help you by giving you the money for the down payment." My conditioned response, when someone offers to do something extremely unusual, is, "No, that's all right, we can make it." After I said this, his line was supposed to be, "Oh, I insist! We want you to take it." Unfortunately, he did not share the same cultural background. He looked hurt and said, "Oh, I'm sorry. We thought it would help you."

The engaged should appreciate that their backgrounds frequently determine how disagreements are handled. For instance, some people sound the charge, others sound the retreat, and others are immobilized and just stand there. I discovered this some years ago when I met a Cheshire grin. During an interview a wife became increasingly upset. I had lost visual contact with her husband and asked her what was the matter. She explained, "Just look at Darrell. Whenever I become upset, he laughs at me." Without looking at him, I said, "Oh, he would never be laughing at you at a time like this." When she again told me to look at him, I glanced over and saw that he had broken into a very broad grin. When I commented upon this, he denied it, explaining, "I'm not laughing." He was unaware that he became immobilized by anger and tension. Not knowing what to do, he broke into a broad grin.

The same misunderstanding occurs when a churner marries a snorer. A couple may be letting the sun set upon their anger and the churner may be absolutely unable to sleep. As she lies there becoming increasingly upset, she finally turns toward her husband deciding to hash out the problem. Just then, out of the stillness of the night, comes a loud snore "z-z-z." Unless she realizes that he may have learned that withdrawing into sleep is the best thing to do when there is disagreement, she will interpret his snoring as indifference.

It is frequently difficult for a man to relate constructively to a fiancée or wife who is crying. Rather than to appreciate this as a way of showing emotion (if it were socially acceptable, men would also cry), he may walk away saying, "Let me know when you're ready to talk sensibly," or "Don't think you're going to get your way by turning on the floodgates." Most people do not use crying manipulatively. It is just another way of sounding the alarm.

Men seem to grunt rather than cry. When we look like Atlas with the weight of the world on our shoulders, and are asked, "What's wrong?" we often grunt, "Nothing!" We need to remember that *nothing* is often a big hard lump of *something*.

There are many similar little and not-so-little differences that can create serious misunderstandings. Although the specifics of these differences cannot be understood until after marriage, couples can commit themselves to the belief that coming to truly know each other is a life-long process. It is helpful for couples to develop a mental attitude which prepares them for any response. I have asked many newlyweds if they experienced any surprises. Several have responded that he or she "really has some odd habits!"

These odd habits may be our Germanness or Frenchness, which determines whether we squeeze the toothpaste from the bottom or top of the tube, whether we like large or small meals, whether we kiss each other when we leave for work or return home, whether Christmas is celebrated on December 24 or 25, etc.

As the couple is challenged to recognize and bring these differences into the open, each needs to remind himself of the tendency to think, "My way is the only way." As each party begins to appreciate this, he may understand the tendency to interpret a "strange reaction" from his spouse as rejection. To avoid misinterpretation, he or she must be forthright enough to clarify the meaning of behavior which seems unloving. Each must also be aware of the tendency to expect *the other* to change and adjust. Remember, "If you have the urge to alter, don't go to the altar."

One ineffective way in which we often try to make adjustments is to make the other person more like us. For instance, if one is bothered because the other is not talkative, he may talk more in an effort to encourage the other to become more talkative. One could place talking on a scale of 0 - 10, assuming that the talkative partner has a rating of 6 and the other has a rating of 4. The talkative spouse may increase to 7, anticipating the other will then accelerate to 5. Unfortunately, the not-so-talkative spouse may decelerate to 3, hoping to bring the other to 5. When we try to change the other in some subtle and indirect way, we generally end up farther apart. The feelings about differences and desired changes must be brought into the open where each can discuss the extent to which he or she is willing to change for the benefit of the overall relationship. Spouses must also strive to appreciate their differences rather than to try so hard to make everything just the same. For instance, if a very thrifty person marries one whose money burns a hole in his pocket, they may find that the thrifty partner's correction protects them from impulse purchases, but the other's "quirk" causes them to at least purchase what they need.

It is the wise couple who believes that there are several ways to live a Christian marriage. It is the holy couple who prays for the grace to find the way that is best suited to *them* and not to just the *one*.

6

ME AND MY FOIBLES

A danger inherent in any discussion of cultural differences is that the engaged may look at certain differences or imperfections and say, "This is just the way I am and there is *nothing* I can do about it." This unfortunate attitude is very destructive. The truly mature person is able to look at his or her life, identify shortcomings, and firmly resolve to make necessary changes. The wise party asks, "What is it about me that would be difficult to live with?" The falsely self-satisfied and immature individual says, "Take me exactly as I am."

The most critical risk of this chapter is that one may use the ideas as an excuse for avoiding introspection and look only at the other saying, "He sure has described *you*. Now *you* have some idea of what *you* need to change!" This chapter is designed for introspection and not projection.

There are many ways in which people realize their imperfections. For instance, our children helped me become aware of perfection as an imperfection. In spite of our belief that "the family that camps together deserves what they get," we continue to stick to this as the only way we can have vacations away from home. On one trip, while midway through the ordeal of setting up the tent, I was ordering the children to help, exclaiming, "If you don't help, we'll never go camping again." As I said this, the children looked to the heavens, praying that we would, indeed, never camp again. When camp was finally set up, we went on a "big fishing trip." As we approached the dock with our three sunfish, I was faced with the momentous decision of either tying onto the dock or beaching the boat. I decided to beach it, then changed my mind, and grabbed the dock, knocking our son Mike into the lake. Mike, who takes special delight in being hysterical, cried for ten minutes. When he was finally subdued, our youngest son Tim, speaking with a lisp, commented, "Mr. Poifect goofed." From that day, they have kept track of my goofs and occasionally throw them up to *me* when I correct *them.*

As this discussion continues couples will recognize the need to truly confront some problems. Because of the negative societal attitude toward marriage, I had earlier thought it necessary to be very positive, avoiding pesky issues that may cause a couple to think they were not prepared for marriage. This original stance was in opposition to a mental attitude of many marriage educators who seemed to judge their success by the number of couples who decided not to marry. Although that attitude, as well as the general societal attitude, is too negative and pessimistic, couples should look at some characteristics that could alert them to present or potential problems.

Temper and Stubbornness

Temper and stubbornness fall into the category of traits we don't bother to change because we think they are either cute or that ours is the right way. Some may blame their genes for these problems. They may say, "That's my Italian coming out" or "That's my Polish stubbornness."

During the first years of our marriage, I excused my temper, explaining, "This is my Frenchness and you have no right to become upset! It's over as quickly as it starts."

However, in spite of my direct order, Alice did become upset. I finally appreciated that a show of temper was totally alien to her experience.

The strongest exchange between Alice and her parents occurred when she was fifteen. She was twenty minutes late returning to the car after a baseball game. When her father asked, "Where have you been?" Alice replied, "Well, I'm only fifteen minutes late." He said, "Don't talk like that! You're not yet dry behind the ears." Those of us from more vociferous families would smile to think that this was the strongest exchange to occur between a daughter and her parents. However, that background ill-prepared her for a guy who was prone to immature tantrums. I finally realized it was far easier for me to change my immaturity then it would be for her to adjust to it. More important, it would certainly be to my benefit to change.

EXPLETIVES

The language of Americans has degenerated to the point that it is socially acceptable for both men and women to punctuate their conversations with four-letter words. The occasion of bestowing unto each other the sacrament of matrimony is an opportune time to reverse this abusive habit. I swore when I was about six years old and some- one corrected me, explaining, "You can't swear until you're a man." I apparently kept that in mind because I began to "swear like a trooper" when I turned eighteen. As I became more aware of psychology I realized I had a "per- fect cop-out for swearing." Because of my childhood ex- perience, I identified swearing with masculinity. Gradually, I became aware that swearing is inconsistent with Christian living and resolved to change that habit.

POUTING

Prior to marriage the pouting of a fiancé or fiancée may look cute and be joked about. "Up a little bit at the corners, give me a little smile." However, what had been so cute during engagement becomes the deadly silent treatment in marriage.

PARENTAL CONCERNS AND ADVICE

If there is a total disregard for parental concerns or objections about the marriage or if there is an extremely negative attitude toward preparing for marriage through conversations with one's pastor or in a course, one must carefully assess the underlying reasons for such objection. Some very autonomous couples operate upon the premise, "No one can teach me anything about marriage." Others think, "What can a priest, who isn't married, possibly tell me about marriage?" Other very private persons think, "Each marriage is very individual and no one has a right to interfere with it." These judgements say something about one's readiness for marriage. The individual who is fixated upon his own autonomy or the absolute privacy of his life is a risk for the highly interdependent and social relationship of marriage. God has given us the Christian community as a way to learn from each other. One who is closed to learning from the Christian body must overcome the pride underlying such isolation.

JEALOUSY

Jealousy is another emotional response which is often smiled at before marriage. A fiancée may be proud that her husband-to-be becomes jealous of anyone who looks at her. She may feel secure looking upon this possessiveness as an indication of his true love. She may be twice as satisfied if he gets into a fight with someone who talks to her. After marriage this sign of love is viewed with utter disdain and seen as controlling possessiveness precipitated by intense insecurity.

AGE

Certain problems might be suggested by the age at which a couple marries. Couples are generally turned off when they learn that 33 percent of all divorced couples are teen-agers and 62 percent of all divorced men and 75 percent of all divorced women were under twenty-five when married. This is compared with an overall rate for the United States of 4.9 percent per 1,000 population. Although couples do not want to be treated as statistics, they should understand why the divorce rate is alarmingly higher for those who marry young.

One tragedy associated with youthful marriages revolves around that they occur before the interests of either party have stabilized. One's interests at age seventeen or eighteen are a very poor indication of what those interests and goals will be at age twenty-five. Thus, at age eighteen, a couple may seem to share much in common. However, seven years later they may be miles apart. In spite of their initial love for each other, the lack of a common purpose causes them to drift apart. They become increasingly alien from and antagonistic toward each other. They also become very hostile toward themselves for having developed these repugnant feelings toward someone they once loved. It is a sad experience to talk with a young couple who sincerely love each other and intend to marry, and yet a third party realizes how basically different they are and the future price they will pay for these differences.

Other couples may marry at an earlier age because they are in love with love or want to escape an unhappy home situation. Still others may have been very autonomous children and teen-agers and an early decision to marry is another instance in which they call their own shots.

It is equally important for an older engaged couple to seriously look at the age question. Perhaps their interests and goals are so firmly entrenched that they will find it extremely difficult to adapt to each other. This may be especially true for those who enter a second marriage. Those whose marriages have been annulled should be certain they have truly understood the reasons for the break-up of their first marriage and have modified whatever personal behavior led to that break-up.[1] Those who have been widowed also need to be certain they have worked through the very special problems associated with the death of a spouse and widowhood. One of the more perplexing problems is the unconscious tendency to marry to provide a father or mother for children. There is also a tendency to slip into another marriage before the grief caused by the death of the first spouse has been satisfactorily resolved.

Still others may marry at a later age because of a sense of social pressure. Some may enter into an ill-advised marriage after the death of a parent they loved and cared for. Such a marriage represents an indiscreet effort to cope with unresolved grief. It is what age may mean or disguise, and not age itself, that is important.

THE ETERNAL PESSIMIST

Another problem to solve before marriage is that of a Sad Sam or Samantha. Sam and Samantha have poor self-images and operate upon the premise, "When my ship comes in, there will be a dock strike." They have a pessimistic attitude toward life and are seemingly like an accident waiting to happen. They usually wonder, "What can go wrong now?" or "If things are going nicely, can disaster be far behind?" Unfortunately, Sam and Samantha fall into the trap of a self-fulfilling prophecy. Their glum and pessimistic attitude, which predicts disaster, actually begins to cause disaster. When disaster occurs, Sam or Samantha, with an apparent sense of relief, says, "See, what did I tell you? Nothing works out for me."

---

[1] The term annulment recognizes that a Catholic may be remarrying after an initial marriage has been declared null and void by a diocesan tribunal.

This pessimism is generally caused by a poor self-image, which prompts the person to believe that nothing can work out for him. He apparently feels he deserves trouble and strife. This poor image is generally caused by a highly individualized reaction to a unique interaction of developmental experiences combined with inherited traits and characteristics which prompt the person to believe he is unworthy. Sam or Samantha should understand how this destructive self-image developed and be willing to form a plan of action (discussed later) which looks at oneself more positively.

If Sam or Samantha fails to change his or her view of self, successful marriage will be extremely difficult. Not only is it difficult for the other spouse to live with the depression, but the afflicted spouse's disposition will not permit marital success. That the apparent drive for failure is unconscious only makes it all the more insidious. A fiancée may feel, "Sam needs me so badly. I am the only one who can get him out of his moods. I guess it's true that I am the only good thing that has ever happened to him. He will feel so much better after we are married and can be together all the time." If Sam or Samantha's attitude remains unchanged, the burden of living with the depression may become almost unbearable.

DRINKING

The real meaning of drinking is often undermined prior to marriage. One party may recognize that the other abuses alcohol but discounts its importance, thinking, "After we are married and have our own home, drinking will not be nearly as important as it is now." Unless one truly grips the meaning of these behavioral patterns, they will be more, rather than less, punctuated after marriage. The couple who is refinishing furniture for their first apartment recognize that it is tempting (about 1:00 a.m.) to think that the scratches, which they are too tired to sand out, will

be covered by the stain and varnish. Sadly, they realize
that the stain and varnish only magnify the imperfections.
It is the same with marriage. Because of the pressures of
this critical transition in life, personal imperfections and
interpersonal problems become more glaring after marriage.

HASSLES

If a couple is always involved in some hassle, they
should not wait until after marriage to try to understand
the cause of these frequent upsets. Perhaps some of the
thoughts here can help a couple identify the reason for
the chronic conflict. The same warning applies to the
couple whose engagement ring has been worn out by
throwing it back and forth. The couple whose engagement
is on-again, off-again sometimes deludes themselves into
thinking, "Since we always end up back together, we must
truly be meant for each other." That is tragically simplistic.

Some naively believe love will conquer all. Still others
think, "He may not love me, but my love for him will bring
him to loving me." This is a dangerous attitude which
overlooks the reality that some who have never been loved
find it hard to learn to love. Those who have been spoiled
and believe they are the center of the universe find it difficult to learn to truly love another. It is true that we learn
to love *each other* in marriage, but marriage is not the
place to teach one to *learn to love.*

THE CLERGYMAN'S DILEMMA

Some couples may find that a conscientious clergyman
will muster up his courage and gently suggest that one
or both of the partners have a problem which may make
this an inadvisable time to marry. Although this may be
difficult for the couple or one of them to accept, one should
appreciate that the clergyman spends several hours each
week counseling troubled married couples. As he talks

with an engaged couple who is having similar problems, he would be irresponsible if he did not share his concern. The couple must decide how to apply his advice.

Some couples wonder if a clergyman can refuse to witness their marriage. The priest, minister, or rabbi must struggle with his own conscience. If it seems that a couple has the potential for severe problems, some clergy feel obligated to delay their participation in the marriage until the basic problem has been resolved. Others feel they have the obligation to identify the problem, advise help, but in the end do what the couple asks. Others may be terribly doubtful about witnessing the sacrament when one or both of the engaged have little interest in a sacramental life.

The basic answer is, "yes," a clergyman may refuse to witness a wedding at a particular time. In fact, in the Catholic Church, some dioceses require priests to receive special permission from the chancery before witnessing marriages fitting a certain pattern.

Perhaps another word can be said about the conversations a couple preparing for marriage has with a clergyman. They may notice that he seems ill at ease or not exactly certain of his role. Hopefully, the following comments will not come across as a put-down, but engaged couples must consider how *they* come across.

Some engaged couples convey a very omnipotent attitude which is threatening to many who are involved in a ministry or apostolate to the engaged. This may be an age-related phenomenon or a defense which the engaged use to disguise their own fears. Another phenomenon typical of many engaged is that they experience difficulty carrying a conversation. This complicates the job of the clergyman who relies upon conversation to carry out his ministry.

Clergy generally find their work with the engaged — especially helping couples who truly want to receive the sacrament of marriage from each other — a most rewarding dimension of their ministry.

AN APPROACH TO CHANGE

If one has been introspective and open enough to recognize some imperfections and brave enough to work on the necessary changes, some basic steps can be followed to effect change. On the natural level, it is helpful to follow the slogan:

It's easier to act one's way into new ways of thinking than to think one's way into new ways of acting.

This implies that we often fail to change because we only think about it and fail to take necessary action.

Realizing that success builds upon success, the best way to effect change is to have successful experiences with change. For example, if one finds bad temper or jealousy interfering with intra or interpersonal happiness, manages to control the adverse tendencies, and finds that the relationship then goes more smoothly, one will recognize reward and be inclined to continue the modified behavior. Most New Year's resolutions are doomed to failure because people too often think about change but do not effect change.

If one comments that he will try to change a particular habit, such as stubbornness, generally that effort will fail. The expression "try to change" is a convenient cop-out. After one has inevitably failed and fallen back into the same old rut, he can comfortably say, "Well, I told you I would try and that's all you can expect." The more we fail, the more convinced we are that change is impossible. "This is the way I am, and you'll have to accept me as I am."

If a person has identified the particular habit or behavioral pattern he or she desires to modify, it is advisable to write this down and enter daily adjustment notations on a chart. We have a greater chance of success if we are accountable to something (a notebook, chart, or graph) and to someone (a spouse, fiancé or fiancée, pastor, coun-

selor, or confessor). It is also helpful to reward progress
through a little favor that one can do for the other.

As problems for some people are sufficiently deep
and entrenched, professional counseling may be advised.
Some will believe that they cannot afford this before marriage. However, such help can only become more expensive in human terms after marriage.[2] Yet, the idea that a
problem is deeply entrenched can serve as another cop-out.
Many people enter into counseling only to prove they
cannot be helped. Before one can do anything, he must
actually decide to change as distinct from *considering*
change or *trying* to change. One purpose of counseling
is to help the person decide to change. This decision is
the most basic, fundamenal, and essential step.

BEYOND THE NATURAL LEVEL

The believing Christian couple is not limited by only
natural powers. They may ask our Lord to enter their
lives in a very special way. They may pray that the Spirit

---

[2] A clergyman or physician generally can recommend competent counselors and therapists. Many dioceses offer premarriage and marriage counseling services under the auspices
of Catholic Social Services. There are other agencies, such as
Lutheran Social Service and Family and Children Service, as
well as many marriage and family counselors in private practice.

It is helpful to appreciate the difference between premarriage education and premarriage counseling. Premarriage
education includes sharing information that will help a couple
plan their wedding and prepare for marriage. It assumes that
the couple has no significant blocks to receiving this information. Premarriage counseling recognizes that some emotional
blocks in people do interfere with truly preparing for marriage.
These blocks may contraindicate marriage. Premarriage education involves direct teaching and counseling and includes the
effort to understand the behavior or attitude which seemingly
interferes with the prospect of a rewarding marriage. Once the
dynamics are understood, a plan is developed for modifying
the apparently dysfunctional attitude or behavior.

will grant them an understanding of why they experience a certain tension in their relationship or why one partner or the other feels a sense of "dis-ease." Then, once he or she decides to change, one can avail himself of the power of supernatural grace. Fortunate is the recovering alcoholic who has admitted his own powerlessness and turned to the Supreme Being for help. For the Christian, this implies turning to Jesus. Those Christians, for whom confession is a part of their religion, should not overlook the power of this sacrament. Jesus loves the person who admits his faults (as distinct from rationalizing them as neurotic hang-ups), is contrite, and asks for his help to change.

One can only sympathize with young Catholics in their formative years during the tumultuous 1960s and early 1970s. Perhaps they never had the opportunity to experience the power of the sacrament of penance, which reconciles us with ourselves, our brothers, and our Lord and Savior. New rites have been developed for penance, a sacrament which will again rise to prominence within the Church. The Catholic couple or party will do themselves a favor if they talk with their priest about the rediscovered meaning of penance and avail themselves of this sacrament.

Couples would also be remiss if they did not realize the power of the Eucharist. One who is bothered by inner hurts should realize that at Communion our Lord invites us to ask for a healing of hurts or painful memories. Of course, before supernatural grace can work within us, we must permit it to work. Since God will not impose himself upon us, the troubled person can render him as ineffective as any clergyman or counselor.

DOES RELIGION MAKE A DIFFERENCE?

The discussion of the power of our faith, cultural up-bringing, and interpersonal differences certainly calls upon the conscientious couple to talk about the importance of religion in their lives. One feels sympathy for those who were brought up within the Catholic Church in the post-Vatican II era. People of other faiths were affected by what was happening within that Church as well as what was happening within the larger society. During the 1960s and 1970s, we reexperienced a "God is dead" era in which we honored the technological achievements of man rather than the glory of God. It was "sophisticated" to assume an attitude of "God may be all right for those who need him, but I don't, so bug off." Some students in parochial schools were caught in the midst of such controversy between faculty, parents, Church, and school. Some decided, "If you people can't get things together any better than this, my relationship will be only with God and not with an institutional Church."[3]

Since engagement is a time of critical transition, it is advisable to assess the meaning God and formal religion has to the engaged. It may also be a time to reconcile oneself with God and his Church. If things go better with Coke, think of the difference God and his Church can make! If religion means nothing to either of the betrothed, it may not present an interpersonal conflict for them. However, they will experience that void in their lives which can only be filled by an awareness of God and the desire of his Son to be a part of their lives.

A couple must seriously consider not marrying when one partner is interested in a truly sacramental union and the other could care less. We are noticing an increasing number of engagements in which one party identifies himself as an atheist or agnostic and the other as a truly believing and practicing Christian. The agnostic or atheist may have fallen away from his Church. The believer truly wants the marriage witnessed in the Church and hopes his or her faith will be strong and meaningful enough to encourage the other to join or return to the Church.

---

[3] I thank Fr. John Forliti, Office of Education of the St. Paul and Minneapolis Archdiocese, for sharing these thoughts.

In some respects these marriages resemble those of the early Christians who married pagans who later converted to Christianity, but there is one dramatic difference, the pagans had not been exposed to Christianity. Thus, they had not actually rejected it. In contrast, many of the new pagans are Christians who have cast aside that belief. It is one phenomenon to not embrace something about which one knows very little and quite another to angrily reject something that had been an integral part of one's life.

Perhaps this only underscores the important role of the clergyman in preparing a couple for marriage. An "atheistic" party may be caught in the popular rejection of God and may not have given serious thought to this action. There may also have been some combination of hurtful experiences causing the person to tune out the institutional Church and, in the process, begin referring to himself as an athiest. But, if after conscientious pastoral counseling, the pagan partner adheres to his position, the couple must recognize that to proceed with the marriage is to invite future unhappiness. They will not share a part of life which is so meaningful to one partner that he or she hopes that the effects of marriage combined with the grace of God will cause a conversion.

THE INTERFAITH MARRIAGE

The interfaith marriage is an extremely sensitive issue. A decade or two ago most religions strongly disapproved of interfaith marriages. Thus, they occurred infrequently. Yet, many interfaith couples have built exemplary Christian lives, and an insensitive application of certain rules has created unnecessary hurt for many loving couples.

An interfaith marriage has become more the rule than the exception. Some feel concern today that they are encouraged too much. Some are concerned that the congratulatory attitude extended to the interfaith couple suggests, "Congratulations for having overcome the hang-ups of a previous era and for braving a new frontier of religious tolerance." Perhaps the increased incidence of interfaith marriages is due both to a certain sense of religious indifference as well as to the ecumenical emphasis.

The engaged need to appreciate the impact of the cultural differences inherent in their "Frenchness or Germanness." The practice of religion is also a part of our cultural upbringing and is deeply inculcated within the hearts of those for whom religion is important. The total impact of religion is not cast aside simply because it is the mod thing to do. Those who think they can do this may be fooling themselves.

Some others may have a naive understanding of ecumenism. Rather than to realize that the ecumenical movement is directed toward an understanding and discussion of the differences between the various religions, some believe it means there is no difference between the various religions or that the differences are only accidental. This attitude is an insult to all religious groups. Without differences there is no reason to have Lutherans, Baptists, Catholics, etc. True ecumenism must honestly discuss the genuine differences. The attitude of some who complain that interfaith marriages are a problem for the Churches, who are too bound up in their self-interest to resolve their differences, is simplistic and unfair to an unaware couple. On the other hand the idea that members of one Christian body are second-class Christians who will join the true Church when they tire of their status is cruel and capricious.

If religion makes any difference to people, an anticipated interfaith marriage presents special problems for a sincere couple. To say that it makes no difference may either represent the sad admission that God makes no difference or it may suggest a naive lack of awareness of the meaning of various religious practices.

During a weekend retreat for engaged couples, a Lutheran woman commented that she always felt badly when she went to Mass with her Catholic fiancé and could not receive Communion. Another person, overhearing the conversation, commented, "You would not need to worry about that in our parish. Our pastor is not hung-up about that." Yet, she was open to the idea that that practice was an insult to both traditions. One symbol of Communion is union, that is, the communicants have a faith union with each other. To say that Catholics and Lutherans are presently in union would be untrue. Certainly, one feels badly about this separation, but little is accomplished by pretending union. The fiancée was impressed that her act of not receiving Communion would have a powerful symbolic message. That is, she served as a symbol to the disunion and provided a clarion call for us to follow the promptings of the Spirit in resolving religious differences.

The sincere interfaith couple will pray about their desire to marry each other. They will explore whether or not it is truly God's will that they enter into marriage with each other. The religiously sincere and loving couple, who arrive at the decision that God *does not* intend that they marry, deserves the highest respect.

In spite of the need to alert couples to the risks of interfaith marriages, one must not become unnecessarily negative. The interfaith couple can certainly develop a meaningful spiritual life which revolves around their mutual effort to be drawn closer to our Lord. They are free to participate in some parts of the formal worship of each other's Church.

Yet, it is helpful to consider the present attitude of the Catholic Church towards the marriage of a Catholic to a member of another Church. At any rate, if permission is granted to the Catholic spouse to enter an interfaith marriage, the couple could then ask for the marriage to be witnessed in the church of either spouse.

Special permission is required for a Catholic to marry a person of another faith. It is necessary for the Catholic partner (through a priest) to receive the bishop's permission. This suggests that the attitude is hesitant and reluctant. The Church is essentially saying it wishes it were otherwise, but if certain conditions are present, it will grant its blessing.

The attitude is consistent with that which has been traditionally expressed by the various Christian Churches. Also, Judaism has strongly disapproved of intermarriage with non-Jews. Their survival as a distinct religious and ethnic group may be due to the observance of this policy. The language of Moses in Deuteronomy 7:1-3 advises: "When the Lord, your God, brings you into the land which you are to enter and occupy.... Make no covenant with them.... You shall not intermarry with them,..." The concern about interfaith marriages is based upon the realization that mixed marriages frequently result in a weakened Church membership or no involvement at all in the religious group. Frequently, the children born of interfaith marriages tend to make mixed marriages themselves and have less Church involvement than children born to parents of the same religion. These reasons will, no doubt, continue to be relevant. One cannot be certain whether the concern about a higher percentage of divorce in interfaith marriages will continue to be relevant. The divorce rate has become so escalated that it is difficult to identify *a* particular cause. Today, differences over religion may not be so much a factor in divorce as the failure of religion to play a prominent role in the spouses' lives. However, it remains true that interfaith marriage increases the range and variety of family problems.

If the Catholic Church grants permission for an interfaith marriage, the Catholic partner is required to promise (verbally or written) that he will do all within his power to maintain his own faith and to rear the children as Catholics. No promise is asked of the non-Catholic partner. The phrase "all within his power" can prove ambiguous. Does it mean, "Well, I talked with my fiancé about rearing the children Catholic and he refuses, but I did all within my power."? In this situation it seems the marriage would be contraindicated because the one party refuses to keep the promise. If the refusal to cooperate occurs postmaritally, the Catholic spouse would need to seek pastoral advice to determine what constitutes "all within one's power." This certainly demonstrates why this issue should be faced pre rather than postmaritally.

In discussing the faith to be shared with their children, the sincere couple should not cave into the popular attitude, "I don't believe in shoving religion down the throats of children. They should be free to choose whichever religion appeals to them. We are going to wait until the children are sixteen and then permit them to choose the Church they prefer." Parents who operate upon this premise do a serious disservice to their children. Neither will the sincere interfaith partner say, "Since children are taught religion by their mothers, we will bring ours up in the Church of their mother." The Christian partner would not use this cop-out as a way of avoiding his duty.

A person should not undermine the nature of the differences between the Churches. An interfaith couple can develop a meaningful spiritual life. The promise of the Catholic partner to do all within his power to maintain his own faith and to rear the children as Catholics should be thoroughly understood. Beyond this, St. Paul's words in Ephesians 4:3-6 remind us of our goal:

> There is but one body and one Spirit, just as there is but one hope given all of you by your call. There is one Lord, one faith, one baptism; one God and Father of all, who is over all, and works through all, and is in all.

Perhaps this discussion suggests that the engaged of the same faith should not be smug and self-satisfied. They are challenged to be certain that their shared faith will actually make a difference in their marriage. When faith is integrated into a couple's life, the existence of certain values will preclude various problems. Yet, the key word is integrated. Although spouses may be nominal members of the same Church, the failure to truly integrate their faith into their daily lives prevents them from cooperating with God's grace in creating the marriage available to the couple who truly believes and practices the message of the Gospel.

FOR DISCUSSION

1. Have you noticed any tendency to slip into a pattern of taking each other for granted, becoming careless about your relationship, and/or accentuating the negative rather than the positive?

2. What reactions did you receive when you announced your engagement? Was there any gentle harassing which made it difficult to truly celebrate the engagement?

3. Have you previously considered the dramatic difference between secular and Christian marriage? What meaning does this difference have to you?

4. Do you understand the types of church marriages discussed and have you considered entering a truly sacramental union?

5. What is the distinction between fighting out and resolving disagreements?

6. What positive ways have you found to deal with differences and to what extent do you continue to deal with differences destructively?

7. How does the HALT approach apply to you?

8. What discussion have you had concerning the differences in your life-styles?

9. What differences and similarities are there in your family backgrounds?

10. What is the attitude of your parents toward your engagement? Have you, or would you, consider asking for parental permission to marry and, if that permission is granted, asking for your parents' blessing?

11. Have you identified some particular personal difficulty that should be resolved prior to marriage?

12. What are the strengths in your engaged relationship? What are the problem areas upon which you should be working?

13. How has pride interfered with resolving interpersonal and/or intrapersonal difficulties?

14. Have you noticed that it is the apparently small things that cause more upset than the important issues in life?

15. If you are entering an interfaith marriage, have you discussed the impact the faith difference will have in your lives?

SUGGESTIONS FOR READING

The Teaching of Christ — A Catholic Catechism for Adults. Huntington, Indiana: Our Sunday Visitor Press, 1976.

This comprehensive volume offers a synthesis of Christian revelation and human life and a guide to the meaning of Christian life today.

Berne, Eric. *Games People Play.* New York: Grove Press, 1964.

One of the first books that popularized transactional analysis, it helps those who want to understand the intricacies of interpersonal relationships.

Bird, Joseph and Lois. *Marriage Is for Grown-ups.* Garden City, NY: Doubleday and Co., 1969.

A candid analysis of the problem areas which confront every married couple and a discussion of mature rational ways to work toward their solutions.

Blanck, Rubin and Gertrude. *Marriage and Personal Development.* New York: Columbia University Press, 1968.

> Explains that difficulties between marriage partners can be understood when seen as reflecting gaps and failure in development.

Dalton, Katharina. *The Menstrual Cycle.* New York: Pantheon Books, 1969.

> Regarding the menstrual cycle, this book offers women an answer to much of today's unnecessary suffering and offers men an understanding of the problems of women.

Foley, Leonard. *Your Confession: Using the New Ritual.* Cincinnati: St. Anthony Messenger Press, 1975.

> A helpful approach to understanding the sacrament of reconciliation.

Greenburg, Dan. *How to Be a Jewish Mother.* Los Angeles: Pierce, Stern, Sloan Pub., Inc., 1964.

> A delightfully humorous book for those interested in how cultural differences can affect a marriage.

Harrington, Jeremy. *Your Wedding: Planning Your Own Ceremony.* Cincinnati: St. Anthony Messenger Press, 1974.

> Provides a checklist and several suggestions for planning the wedding ceremony.

Harris, Thomas. *I'm OK; You're OK: A Practical Guide To Transactional Analysis.* New York: Harper and Row, 1967.

> A helpful approach to understanding and resolving some difficulties experienced in relationships.

McHugh, James T. (Ed.). *Marriage in the Light of Vatican II.* Washington: Family Life Division, United States Catholic Conference, 1968.

> A discussion of the insights Vatican II offered for Christian marriage.

McHugh, James T. *Mixed Marriage: New Directions.* Washington: Family Life Division, United States Catholic Conference, 1971.

A book intended for the couple entering an interfaith marriage.

McNutt, Francis. *Healing.* Notre Dame, IN: Ave Maria Press, 1974.

A discussion of the healing power of faith.

Palmer, Paul. "Shall They Make a Covenant?". *The Priest.* (July-August, 1975), pp. 14-19.

Discusses the difference between a contract and covenant.

Quesnell, John G. *Marriage: A Discovery Together.* Notre Dame, IN: Fides Publishers, Inc., 1974.

Discusses the factors which influence personality development and how these can affect marriage positively or negatively.

Schillebeeckx, E. *Marriage: Human Reality and Saving Mystery.* New York: Sheed and Ward, 1965.

A classic source book regarding the theology of marriage.

Volledregt, G. N. *The Bible on Marriage.* De Perre, WI: St. Norbert Abbey Press, 1965.

An analysis of the biblical comments concerning marriage.

Whalen, William J. *Separated Brethren.* Huntington, IN: Our Sunday Visitor, Inc., 1972.

A brief and helpful commentary on the essentials of most religious traditions.

SECTION II

THAT THE TWO
SHALL BECOME ONE

7

FROM WOMAN'S LIB
TO ADAM'S RIB[1]

One of the challenges facing Christian couples involves coming to grips with the meaning of equality, developing an approach to decision making, and understanding the nature of authority. In considering the subject "That Two Shall Become One," couples will be asked to consider the masculine and feminine models with which they identify, the nature of freedom, the IT'S and DIS of marriage, three different ways in which couples make decisions, and the type of authority that is needed within marriage. As couples begin to explore the meaning of this first challenge to Christian marriage, they should realize that some of the suggested ideas will be diametrically opposed to the popular emphasis.

Burt Reynolds vs. Jesus Christ

Although many men have been angered by woman's liberation, few have asked to what extent they and their

[1] I am grateful to *Our Family* magazine for permitting me to include here some of the ideas originally published in the April and May 1975 issues.

forebears participated in its conception. In the next few pages fiancés are asked to answer some penetrating questions and challenges. The institutionalization of the double standard permitted men to abuse their headship, which many believe God intended them to assume. Not only the double standard, which demands one standard of behavior for men and quite a higher standard for women, but also a misguided sense of masculinity caused men to abuse this God-given responsibility. Thus, drinking to excess and sexually exploiting women were not only permitted by the double standard but also they were considered the mark of a true man. In the name of business some men consume more than a few martinis during two-hour luncheons or eight-hour dinner meetings. In the name of "I've got to earn a living for the family," men have gone on weekend hunting and fishing (business) trips. Resentful wives were quickly reminded, "It's no fun for me either, but that's the way things go in the business world." Wives could only feel terribly guilty that their husbands had to endure the hardships of luncheons, dinners in plush restaurants, and the rigors of hunting and fishing trips.

All this was done in the name of putting bread on the table and shoes on the children. On top of this, husbands reacted in a demeaning fashion toward their wives' work. Many let it be known that they could not be bothered with the nitty-gritty tasks of tending to stopped-up plumbing, runny noses, or a wife who needed tender loving care. Since men were charged with "earning the money," they could not be bothered with the zilchy tasks of life. They have neglected Christ's words that man does not live by bread alone.

Some men fail to realize that the word "virtue" stems from the Latin "*vir*" meaning man. How unfortunate that virtuousness is considered only a feminine trait. Not realizing that manliness is synonymous with virtuousness, some men have condoned hunting trips, stag parties, and endless hours of watching Saturday, Sunday, and Monday football as "the things men do." Unfortunately, the model for masculinity has been inspired by the secular world (Burt Reynolds, John Wayne, Matt Dillon, Joe Namath, John D. Rockefeller, etc.) and not by Christ's teaching. This is exemplified by the fiancé who was embarrassed to tell his friends he was going to attend a pre-Cana retreat. Because of his vagueness, his friends concluded he was involved in a clandestine affair. When his fiancée asked why he could not tell them that he would be on a retreat, he explained, "Oh, I could never admit that." It's a peculiar set of values that makes it more acceptable to "cheat on one's partner" than to spend a weekend in intimate contact with our Lord.

Whenever husbands were questioned about the way they fulfilled their duties, the "Christian husband" was prepared to cite St. Paul's letter to the Ephesians:

> Wives should be submissive to their husbands as if to the Lord because the husband is head of his wife just as Christ is head of his body the church, as well as its savior. As the church submits to Christ, so wives should submit to their husbands in everything (Eph. 5:22-24).

Unfortunately, he preferred to ignore the next verse:

> Husbands, love your wives, as Christ loved the church He gave himself up for her (Eph. 5:26).

This implies more than simply laying down a physical life for a family. It means that a husband and father gives himself as a total gift to his family and lives his life for their benefit. Their welfare is always utmost in his mind. One could also turn to 1 Peter 5:1-4 where leaders of the spiritual community are advised to serve and not be served. Again, in 1 Peter 3:7, men are told that in living with their wives, they must recognize that women are the weaker sex. Men must treat them with respect because women also will receive, together with men, God's gift of life.

The failure of men to accept this teaching helps one to understand why the word "submissive" distresses the engaged who have been hurt by living in a society which ignores it and a family where the father fails to obey it. If husbands followed the advice of Paul and Peter, women would have no need to seek "liberation from chauvinistic males."

If we want to assume the challenge of masculinity, we must stray from the secular world's definition and look to what Christ expects of men. We are called to love our families, exercise spiritual leadership, and share with them the Bread of Life and not meer stones (Matthew 7:9-11 and Luke 11:11-13). Unfortunately, this important task of religious education has generally been abdicated by fathers and assumed by mothers. Spirituality is identified as a feminine and not a masculine trait. Teaching children to pray and joining with them in prayer has become the mother's joyful experience. Unfortunately, too many men give their children the impression that God's last name is Dammit.

The man who desires to be Christ-like will recall that Jesus always sought the will of the Father. He was a man of prayer who went into the desert for forty days before he stepped into the world. He opened himself so God could speak to him and so he could understand his Father's will.

Next, our Lord picked up with a group of fishermen. Many men might think that was a good idea until they realize he took the men away from fishing, made them apostles, and taught them to draw people closer to him so that in coming to know him they could come to know his Father. He then went about teaching and healing. If a fiancé were to take the life of Jesus seriously, he would pray for the strength to be submissive to the will of the Father and to walk more closely with Jesus.

The societal definition of masculinity has made it difficult for husbands to assume Christ-like headship. Instead of being Christ-like leaders assuming headship, some men have been chauvinistic secularists who have assumed "boss-ship," which causes a master-serf relationship as exemplified by Napoleon's comment that "Woman is given to man to bear children; she is therefore his property as the tree is the property of the gardener." How unfortunate that we have identified headship with *boss-ship* rather than *servant-ship*.

The old Jackie Gleason "Honeymooner" TV series or the more recent "All In The Family" or "The Jeffersons" provide excellent examples of chauvinistic boss-ship. Gleason, as Ralph Cramden, once exclaimed, "I am the lord and master! I am everything! You are nothing! You will do what I say, a man's home is his castle, I am everything, you are nothing!" Alice Cramden put her hands on her hips and replied, "Big deal! That makes you king of nothing!" Unfortunately, many bosses cause their wives to feel like nothing.

Happily, the interaction of forces within our society is helping many men become more sensitive human beings, more concerned with enhancing the dignity of their wives. Unfortunately, in an effort to enhance this dignity, many men have continued to confuse boss-ship with Christ-like authority, actually ending up rejecting headship when only intending to reject boss-ship. It is imperative that engaged couples discuss the difference between boss-ship and head-ship.

Of course, the pressure of woman's lib has caused some men to more rigidly assume their role as boss. Others have not known how to react to women experiencing a range of choices broader than marriage, home, and Church. They have been forlorn by the disappearance of various stereotyped notions of masculinity and femininity. As much as women have been hurt by the abuses of masculine authority, men have also experienced the pain of tyrannical authority. Not wanting to be dictators and not clearly understanding authority, many men have abdicated their proper role.

We have let the confusion caused by recent social changes prevent us from moving more closely toward the ideal expressed in:

Creation Of Woman From The Rib of Man
She is not made of his head to top him;
Nor out of his feet to be trampled upon
By him; but out of his side to be equal with
Him; under his arm to be protected; and near
His heart to be beloved.

Yet, considerable progress has been made since I asked my dad why he and his friend always sat in the front seat of the car and my mother and her friend in the back. My father replied, "If your mother's going to drive, it's best that she be in the back seat." We have come some distance from the days in which rigid lines were drawn between the world of the man and the world of the woman.

This difference occurred to Alice and me in the mid-1960s after entertaining some friends. The next day it dawned upon us that after dinner both the husbands and wives went into the living room (rather than separate parts of the home as had been true earlier in our marriage), sat down, and discussed relevant issues. We realized we all had shared the same interests. It also occurred to us that the women were better informed than the men. It seems that wives are assuming responsibility for the liberal education of their families. Many husbands live in a highly specialized and technical world in which they seem to learn more and more about less and less. At times they are not exposed to the broader vicissitudes of life. It is the wives who become involved in community affairs and who do most of the reading. Thus, it would be unwise for a man to believe that "women know little about the affairs of the world." Not only would this attitude cause him to make ill-informed decisions, but his wife would be

denied the opportunity to feel she was fully contributing
to the viability of the marriage.

THE DUAL-CAREER MARRIAGE

Unfortunately, change frequently causes us to swing
to an extreme position rather than strike a helpful balance.
Fifteen years ago, a woman could proudly announce that
she was a homemaker. At present, all too many women
apologetically explain, "I'm just a homemaker." During a
seminar one woman was assigned a subject entitled "On
Being The Total Woman." After her presentation the audi-
ence seemed aware that a total woman was unmarried,
thought children a drag, and had a Ph.D. Considering the
media's impact, one must ask if a modern fiancée truly
may choose homemaking as a career. At retreats many
fiancées exclaim, "I am going to be more than just a homemaker." In exploring this statement, one realizes that they
have been sold four stereotypes regarding homemaking:

1. A homemaker sits at home in front of the TV
   eating candy,
2. Any work outside the home is more rewarding
   than homemaking,
3. A homemaker is involved in meaningless volunteer
   activities,
4. Children are a drag, no one ought to have them,
   and if one does, 24-hour-a-day nurseries should
   care for them.

Although a few homemakers meet the above criteria,
many more feel fulfilled in their vocation and contribute
meaningfully to society. The Christian homemaker works
to improve the quality of life in her family's immediate
community. She is motivated by goals which transcend
the purely temporal or selfish.

Essentially, a modern fiancée needs permission to choose
homemaking as a career and needs an opportunity to hear
from the many homemakers who believe their career is

rewarding. The popular term "dual-career marriage" suggests that both the husband and wife pursue careers outside the home and share household responsibilities equally. In spite of the proclaimed potential of this arrangement, it places a severe hardship upon marriage and family life. If one spouse does not have primary responsibility for homemaking, it receives the second-class status intimated by the very connotation of "dual-career marriage." Many seem to forget that the marriage in which the husband has his career and the wife pursues homemaking is also a dual-career marriage. After all, homemaking itself is a career!

Naturally, we must realize that countless women have "dual-career lives." They have worked outside the home prior to bearing children, pursued a career at home until the children were grown, and then returned to a career outside the home.

How unfortunate is the expectant mother whose only concern is to quickly return to her job. How much happier she would be if she anticipated the opportunity to be home with the child to whom she could truly give herself. I grieve for the secretary of an obstetrician who induced her labor on a Friday evening and she returned to work two weeks later.

A great wrong is done to many competent young women who desire to mother their children. Because of the emphasis of the media and the vocal discontent, they seem unaware of the women who enjoy the traditional role of wife and mother. Vast numbers of educated and intelligent women who have led promising careers still find motherhood a more rewarding call. It is unfair for the feminists to encourage women to "rise above" their maternal instincts and return to work. A woman's liberation should imply that women can feel confident in themselves as both women and mothers. Women should not be ashamed to glory in being women or enjoy what is unique to women, such as motherhood. All this, of course, says nothing of the benefit to children who have a full-time homemaker as a mother.

As much as one may sympathize with the man whose masculine identity emanated from a long line of Burt Reynolds films and a tradition of institutionalized chauvinism which denied him the opportunity to be truly virile (virtuous), one can now sympathize with the woman whose exposure to popular feminism may deny her the opportunity to truly experience femininity.

Some husbands place their wives in a difficult bind. They want their wives to be full-time homemakers and they also want them to put money into the coffers. Many wives would like to be full-time homemakers but find that their husbands ridicule them for spending all the money and not contributing any. These husbands want the best of two worlds — a comfortable home, good meals, and yet the benefit of their wives' incomes. It is this that causes some women to comment, "Any wife who is forced to work is not liberated." The husband who puts his wife in this bind might become aghast on his tenth wedding anniversary that she is not the same woman he married. It is this husband who exclaims, "What have I done to cause this terrible change in her?"

Essentially, both men and women are called upon to be Christ-like. Each should turn to the saints (rather than to those who have walked only in the world), identify the saint who led a life which resembles the life he or she would like to lead, learn about this saint, and then seek to walk with Christ as did that saint. It seems unfortunate that modern Catholic brides have abandoned the practice of a generation ago when, at the conclusion of the wedding Mass, the bride placed a bouquet at the altar of the Blessed Virgin, symbolizing her prayer that she be granted the grace to be obedient to the Father as was Mary when she responded to the angel, "I am the handmaiden of the Lord." This same spirit of submission enabled her to stand at the foot of the Cross of our Lord and give up her Son in obedience to the Father. Perhaps because of our chauvinistic past grooms have not prayed at the altar of St. Joseph that they also might be submissive to the Father's will. Perhaps, as the double standard is eliminated, both bride and groom will ask for the gifts of submission and obedience.

8

WHY MALE AND FEMALE

Unless couples can agree upon a basic ideological framework, it is extremely difficult to agree upon answers to questions revolving around equality, liberation, and leadership. Because of the intense sensitivity surrounding any discussion of the inherent differences between men and women, it is almost impossible to truly understand one's sexuality. If one begins to discuss sexual differences, he is immediately faced with wondering whether the differences are culturally imposed or innate. Women are given the impression that to be somebody they need to be more like a man than a woman.

A decade ago it was possible to suggest that every woman's nature revealed the feminine characteristics of motherliness, compassion, and endurance. One could suggest that a woman realized fulfillment and became whole when others found wisdom in her intuitive intellect and sensitivity. Also, she withered away or rebelled when her uniqueness as a woman was denied and when she was merely used by the other sex. In the same vein perhaps man's nature revealed the masculine characteristics of being a thinker, builder, leader, competitor, protector, and fighter. Perhaps, too, his natural bent toward working and subduing the earth would degenerate into exploitation and utilitarianism if it were not for his ability to feel the goodness of things. Man's technical power and scientific accomplishments without an accompanying feminine sense of beauty and wisdom would degenerate into weakness.[1] Rather than brush aside these comments as remnants of a chauvinistic past, we need to look seriously at them in an effort to understand God's reasons for creating us as male and female. Although it is difficult to identify innate differences, there are some basic differences between men and women which should not be identified as deficiencies. I find little, however, to support some traditional lists of differences, such as men being more logical and women more intuitive, men more rational and women more emotional.

The adamant stand of the feminists makes it difficult for couples to grip the impact of their sexuality. If all differences are learned and not intended by the Creator, why do men and women marry? Why did God create us as men and women? Or, are some of the liberationists correct? Should opposite sexness not be a requirement for marriage? Some advocate marriage between those of the same sex claiming that only a man can fully understand the sexual needs of a man and only a woman can understand the sexual needs of a woman. Are there psychological differences and is there the psychology of a man and the psychology of a woman? Are differences between the sexes more than physical? What did our Father intend? Are men really to lead in the temporal world? Does his order call for Jesus to be submissive to God, man submissive to the Lord, and wife submissive to her husband? Is fulfillment really to be found by being in proper order with the Divine Plan? Or, is the man right who angrily exclaimed, "You're crazy if you think there is any divine intention that wives are to be submissive to husbands!"?

---

[1] Conrad W. Baars, *A Priest for All Seasons, Masculine and Celibate,* (Chicago: Franciscan Herald Press, 1972), pp. 24-32.

Engaged couples are invited to discuss the idea that *the* differences are more than physical and more than culturally ascribed. In marriage couples form a micro-community in which their differences complement one another. The person totally committed to the secular world will accept a much different answer to the above questions than will the truly committed Christian.

WHERE DO I FIND MY IDENTITY?

Persons from each world are concerned about identity and fulfillment, but their understanding of these concepts will be radically different. The secularist may be self-centered and the Christian strives to be Christ-centered. For the secularist fulfillment involves fulfilling one's own will. The Christian, however, seeks to understand God's will. The secularist may find his identity through a job outside the home, a new automobile, or an extramarital affair. How different for the Christian whose identity comes from Christ. Perhaps we are called to be like St. Theresa who explained, "I have no me, but Christ." Or St. Paul who says, "It is no longer I that live, but Christ in me."

A priest once explained that while he and his twin brother were growing up, they were continually confused with each other. He was sometimes credited with his brother's homeruns and other times with his errors. This provided a model for his priesthood. He prayed he would live his priesthood in such a Christ-like fashion that when he died, our Father would look at him and say, "You look exactly like my Son, please enter." How different this is from the person who loses his freedom to things or to the pursuit of freedom. The person who is only conforming to a popular movement, reacting to a traumatic memory, or fearful of losing his identity is terribly enslaved. The person seeking freedom in a secular sense experiences chronic frustration. He is rebellious when his wishes are not granted and dissatisfied when they are.

The Canadian bishops explained that it would be wrong to think that the persons most free are those who do not believe at all. Knowing what God has established for the fulfillment of man is a freeing principle, not an enslaving one. "The more we know about God's will for us, the more fulfilled we are, the surer we are that we will not destroy ourselves and wander into paths which will not enhance our liberty but take it away entirely. 'The truth will make you free.'" Freedom is not the right to do what we want, but the power to do what we ought. This sense of identity is more comforting than that experienced by the individual who spends so much time defending himself that he does not have an opportunity to become himself.

FIGHTING IT OUT

In fact, the master-serf relationship is not as much a concern today as the horrendous power struggles that modern couples experience. Since spouses are concerned about *their own* identity and doing what *they* want, they become enmeshed in strangulating arguments bent upon proving their point and getting their way rather than working out what is good for the two of them. They are so concerned about their personal identity that they fail to develop a couple identity. To watch couples involved in this is similar to watching two people fence. They parry back and forth until one scores a touché. At the score, they drop their hands, bow their heads, return to a fencing position, and continue until another touché. Because of their intense desire to get their way, the fight becomes the thing. To these Tareyton couples, who would rather fight than switch, the show of power is of utmost importance.

These couples become involved in a zero sum game — Mexican standoff — in which intimacy does not stand a chance. They are unable to admit that the other may have a point worth heeding. To make such an admission would give the other spouse a point in the all-around competition.

In fact, competitive spouses would be unable to apologize to each other. That would be to admit error and give the other spouse a point. In a deeper sense competitive spouses are even prohibited from accepting an apology. Since some consider the admission of error to be virtuous behavior, the apology could not be accepted because that would admit that the other had apologized, giving the apologizing spouse two points in the all-around competition. How unfortunate that they fail to realize that if they fought each other less, they could love each other more.

One can easily see that these relationships offer no opportunity for intimacy. How can you feel emotionally close to your enemy? To sleep together one would have to keep an eye open for an attack. In the competitive marriage one sees the meaning of the quip that competition brings out the best in products but the worst in people. Spouses must appreciate that whenever there is a winner, there must also be a loser. Whenever a spouse believes he has won an argument, he can be assured that the relationship loses. If spouses did not need to win, they would not have to lose. These couples follow the advice of the football coach who proclaimed, "Winning isn't everything, it's the only thing."

The competitive couple places a super emphasis upon being right. The sense of judgment hangs heavier in their kitchens than in most courtrooms. They fail to appreciate the words of Carl Jung, "Where love rules, there is no will to power; and where power predominates, there love is lacking. The one is a shadow of the other." Maturity begins when we are content to feel we are right about something without needing to prove someone else wrong. Competitive couples are very prideful spouses who must admit that rather than argue the principle of the thing, they can dispute the pride of the thing.

The avoidance of intimacy may be a goal of the competitive relationship. In the truly intimate marriage the couple must commit and surrender themselves to each other. They recognize that freedom is always limited by the rights of others as well as by the rights we give away. To be married we give up the right to do just as we please because of concern about our spouse and children. The couple is willing to give up some of these freedoms because he or she thinks that they will find fulfillment in marriage. Thus, on their wedding day the bride and the groom joyfully surrender themselves to one another. A fear of the sexual dimension of marriage can be at the root of a competitive relationship. If one fears intercourse or the surrender that is involved in that relationship, one can safely avoid the conjugal expression of love by continual haranguing.

A readiness to marry implies that one understands his sense of self — who he is. If one basically accepts himself, the stage is set for accepting another. At this time a couple can develop a sense of couple-identity. This demands that couples be concerned about the welfare of the relationship. Thus, although their individual thoughts are extremely important, couples should develop a "we" rather than a "me" approach. They should be concerned about what is good for "us" as well as what is good for "me." This is, of course, difficult for the secular liberationist to accept. Rather than focus on the sense of interdependence necessary for a couple's identity, he emphasizes the need to be independent and "free." The person who focuses only upon his own identity may fail to grasp the sense of oneness expected of the Christian couple who accepts the union Christ has with his Church as the model to emulate. For this reason the committed Christian couple accepts the surname of the husband, which serves to symbolize their unity as well as his leadership.

9

THE IT'S AND DIS OF MARRIAGE

Decision-making, intimacy, and sexual relations depend upon a sense of interdependence, trust, and surrender. As one experiences the dynamic interaction between these characteristics, he also develops an even deeper appreciation of the difference between secular and Christian marriage. The secular world generally believes that decision-making (communication), intimacy, and a satisfying sexual relationship are essential ingredients for a successful marriage. Yet, this world undermines interdependence, trust, and surrender. The undermining is terribly unfortunate because a couple cannot develop an effective system of decision-making, attain intimacy, or achieve a truly satisfying sexual relationship if there is not a sense of interdependence, trust, and surrender.

Unfortunately, the very words *interdependence, trust,* and *surrender* strike alarm in the heart of the "liberated" secularist. This is the unfortunate bind in which the world places couples. It tells them that the primary challenges in marriage revolve around communication, sex, and money. Yet, in suggesting that interdependence, trust, and surrender are undesirable attributes, it denies them the very means to meet the challenges of marriage. One might say:

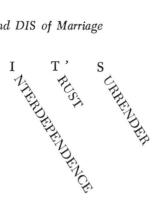

I   T'   S
NTERDEPENDENCE   RUST   URRENDER

NECESSARY FOR

D   I   S
ECISION MAKING   NTIMACY   EXUAL RELATIONS

REASON

Unfortunately, when couples experience tension within their marriage, they generally tune in at the DIS level. That is, they look for some communication technique that will help them make more effective decisions, wonder about the kind of walls that interfere with establishing intimacy, or look for some technique to achieve a more satisfying sexual experience. As long as couples assume this secular approach, they will be unable to effectively come to grips with their marriage.

The Christian views IT'S positively and optimistically, realizing that interdependence is not a characteristic of the neurotic individual who cannot function autonomously. Instead, interdependence expects that one spouse will not make a decision without considering and discussing the effect that decision will have upon the other. If the implementation of that decision will have a negative effect upon the other or upon the relationship, one would have to very seriously consider changing that decision.

Being interdependent means that it is no challenge to be either independent or dependent. One can easily be autonomous or be a dependent "little flower" unable to make the simplest decision. Ask any divorced person how easy it was to develop a sense of independence. Interdependence is a recognition that God has created us as unique individuals and provided us the gift of marriage, which gives us the opportunity to form a small community. In this community we function more effectively as we learn to profit from the talents God has given us.

The interdependent couple recognizes the advantages of making decisions cooperatively. They reject a system of boss-ship in which one person, concerned only with his own wishes and welfare, makes decisions. They reject a boss who is unconcerned with the overall welfare, opinions, and wishes of the family and who runs roughshod over the rights and dignity of others. The interdependent couple is truly liberated because they oppose special interest liberation which interferes with human liberation. They recognize that in marriage independence is equal, dependence mutual, and obligation reciprocal. It is OK to need each other.

Trust makes it unnecessary for either husband or wife to defend themselves. The trusting husband recognizes that his wife would never want to harm him or their relationship. In the same way his wife need not be concerned about her rights, dignity, and integrity as she knows her husband will never want to harm her or their relationship. The development of trust within marriage eliminates competition and opens the door to intimacy.

"Surrender" frightens the secularist as it suggests defeat. In fact, surrender embodies both interdependence and trust. It represents a victory over pride, defensiveness, and fear of opening ourselves to a significant other. We are called upon to surrender in a positive Christian sense and not in a negative secular sense. Christ's crucifixion, the Victory on the Cross, epitomizes how we must surrender to God's will. Our surrender to each other epitomizes a victory over those natural inclinations which cause us to rebel against surrender.

A couple who experiences tension within their relationship should look to the IT'S rather than the DIS level in an effort to discover an explanation for their sense of "DIS-ease." Couples may have difficulty on the IT'S level as a result of earlier childhood experiences which have interfered with their ability to relate interdependently, trust, or surrender to another.

On the other hand, a spouse's investment in his or her life-style may interfere with one's willingness to establish an IT'S relationship. Some couples may operate upon the basis of "my way is best and there is no need for further discussion." Or, a spouse's investment in the popular liberation movement will hamper the ability to relate on this level. Once the reason for resistance to IT'S is uncovered, the couple can talk through the trauma, determining whether or not the fear is relevant. Is it a fear that the afflicted partner is willing to give up? If the resistance is caused by one's investment in a life-style or commitment to a social movement, one could decide whether that commitment is worth the marital dissatisfaction and personal lack of fulfillment.

A couple may only grasp the IT'S level if they are willing to recognize that the Christian message stands in radical opposition to the world. Once the Christian couple recognizes that they view life differently, it becomes easier to accept IT'S, to choose a system of decision-making, and to enjoy a marriage of which our Lord can be a part.

SYSTEMS OF DECISION-MAKING

Couples can essentially choose a system of decision-making based upon one of three models:

1. Authoritative
2. Bastardized-democratic
3. Syncretic-cooperative

After understanding these systems, a couple can discuss the system which they have been using and choose the system they *want to* follow.

The authoritative system results when the insecurity or lack of awareness of one partner prompts him or her to dominate the other. If both want to "be the boss," they fall into a competitive relationship which leaves little room for intimacy.

Others may be fearful of a boss-ship relationship and fall into the trap of a bastardized-democratic system in which they "I don't care each other to death." Since neither wants to shove his opinion down the other's throat, they never share their desires. When asked what they would like to do, they reply, "Whatever you think best." After listening to this for a while, one begins to believe there is a special place in eternity reserved for those without opinions. They may be Peaceful Percys or Priscillas who want, at all cost, to avoid hassles. Unfortunately, when one hears "I don't care" for a couple of years, he begins to believe "She *really doesn't* care!" The "I don't carer" can also blame the other for any wrong decision or do just what he wants, operating upon the premise that "Discussion is a hassle so I will say I don't care and then do exactly what I want."

In some instances one may protest, "But I really don't care." The decision may revolve around the color to paint

the living room, the car to get, where to live, what to eat
for supper, which movie to see, or whether to go out or
stay home. To reply, "I don't care," or "It's up to you,"
can become a cop-out type of automatic response. Even
though we may not care, we must consider that perhaps
we should care. It may be unfair to place all the responsibility for caring on the other. Couples who "I don't care"
each other to death end up sitting around complaining
that life is boring.

My bias favoring a mutual system of decision-making
is evident. This recognizes the talents each partner brings
the marriage. The syncretic-cooperative system recognizes
that couples will make more effective decisions when they
arrive at a solution which is mutually acceptable. This was
a difficult lesson for me, a fairly impulsive should-have-been-
done-yesterday fellow. Alice is a more ponderous person
who is thankful when tomorrow comes but does not get
shook about it.

During the first years of our marriage, I thought, "We
have to make a decision and I can't wait for Alice to make
up her mind." After several lousy decisions I realized I
must not only wait for her but draw her out and help her
contribute to the decision-making process. We now realize
how much is gained from sharing our talents. For instance,
I pride myself on some of my carpentry work. For years
I looked upon this as "man's work" and resisted Alice's
suggestions. After all, what could *she* possibly know about
this? Thankfully, I finally realized she knew a great deal.
An excellent seamstress, her talent has proven useful in
making cabinets, tables, etc. Soon after I started building
a brick wall, I was prepared to throw in the trowel. Then
Alice came to help, finished the wall, and later helped
some friends build a similar wall. The syncretic system
recognizes the unique talents each brings the relationship
and urges them to exercise these talents in a way most
helpful to individual fulfillment and to the cooperative and
interdependent relationship of marriage.

When faced with a decision couples may find it helpful to rate the strength of their opinion on a scale from zero to ten. Thus, if a couple is choosing between living in an apartment or buying a mobile home, the fiancée may exclaim, "I'm not going to live in a mobile home. The mobile home parks are too far out, the initial investment is more than we have, and it will be too difficult to sell if we decide we don't like it. Anyway, I have read that mobile home parks have been devastated during storms. I give a great big zero to a mobile home and a ten to an apartment."

The fiancé may argue, "With an apartment, you only end up with a stack of rent receipts, you have no privacy, and I prefer to have something of our own. I rate the mobile home ten and the apartment zero."

The advantage of the zero to ten scale is that this couple knows they have much more discussion facing them before they can reach a decision. Perhaps they will have to live in a tent for a few months. In most instances, a couple should not make a decision until they are both on the same side of five. Decisions unnecessarily shoved down the throat of the other have a way of backfiring. That car one spouse did not want to buy may get into the "strangest accidents."

EQUALITY AND HEADSHIP

Rather than for a couple involved in an equalitarian marriage to think it is incongruent to also establish identifiable leadership, they should consider that headship is a practical necessity. Spouses who do not decide upon a system of leadership run the risk of falling into a competitive relationship in which there is a struggle for the ill-defined role of leader. Since everyone's responsibility is generally assumed by no one, they can also run the risk of falling into an "I don't care" relationship. Many people have had the experience of checking in with a friend at an airline counter, being given a gate number, proceeding to the concourse, and then turning to each other, simultaneously asking, "What gate is it?" Neither assumed responsibility for listening to the ticket agent.

During the past decade much has been written about the need for consensual decisions. Workshops in decision-making for managers, clergy, superiors of religious orders, and spouses have emphasized the need for involvement on all levels, stressing that people at each strata should have input and decision-making should be mutual. It is interesting that some current literature is questioning that method. Some research is showing that placing the responsibility for decision-making upon one person results in the most effective decisions. Apparently participants in a "group think" do not feel personal responsibility for a decision. Some give in to the general pressure of the group in order to creat a consensus which is artificial. Yet, placing the responsibility for a decision upon one person quickly deteriorates to dictatorship. "Power corrupts and absolute power corrupts absolutely."

First, couples should realistically recognize the need for authority within marriage. That is, one spouse must say, "I will serve as head of this household." This person is not saying that he will make all the decisions but that he will see to it that decisions are made. The other spouse is asked to say, "I will help you assume responsibility as head of this household." A defined leadership is necessary because it is impossible to live in a home in which each goes his own way. In numerous instances couples have disagreed about a life-style when either style would have been consistent with Christian living.

Next, couples should consider that the man assumes responsibility for leadership and that his wife be his helpmate. Does the message of St. Paul (Eph. 5:22-25), which is inspired by God, speak to the modern couple? Does God really intend that the man, submissive to the Lord, is to be the head of his home with his wife submissive to him? Does it belong to natural law that the male is protector, aggressor, and the one who watches over.

If the husband is to head his home, he must exercise a Christ-like leadership. He should never make a decision without consulting his wife and if there were a choice between getting a new shotgun or a new washing machine, he should purchase what was best overall for the family. Headship supplements rather than supplants the dignity of the spouses. The model for the husband is Christ, whose relationship to his Church is not that of slave to master but of lover to beloved. The head of the house does not demand that his orders be followed, as does the boss. Instead, he inspires the family to follow his Christ-inspired lead as Christ inspired his followers to accept his teaching. The husband is to love as did Christ who gave himself up completely to obtain the Church as his bride. In marriage the husband represents the Lord, who did not come to be served but to serve. A husband's love is exemplified by his surrender of self.[1]

If the bride says, "I will help you assume leadership of this family," she is not turning over to her husband the responsibility for all decisions. Although the husband is responsible for making decisions, she will share equally in the decision-making process. This is similar to the relationship a religious has with a superior. The priest, brother, or sister can object to a superior's directive, but if continued discussion does not bring consensus, the superior must make a decision.

Edith Bunker of "All In The Family" is a subjugated and unsubmissive wife. Submission is embraced with the same dignity with which Christ submitted to the Father. It is neither compliance nor capitulation. Unfortunately, many people have thought submission meant being under the thumb of a chauvinistic boss. One woman explained

---

[1] G. Vollebregt, *The Bible on Marriage*, (DePere, WI: St. Norbert Abbey Press, 1965), p. 108.

that she could never be a submissive wife. She had visited a home where the man sat in a chair, directing his wife to turn down the air conditioning, fix him a drink, get him a cigarette, etc. This woman was a serf, not a submissive wife.

Submission is a gift from the Spirit for which one must pray. Once the gift is granted it is only retained through the power of supernatural grace. One cannot fully live the life of the submissive wife with only human powers.

Many wives are reluctant to pray for this gift because they fear that the prayer might be answered. This suggests that one must freely choose submission. We must own our own life, in some sense be free, before we can submit it to another. To do this we must know how God works, be touched by him, have faith in him, and embrace the life we have inherited from him. Healthy submission comes only after one has found independence from human things and has freely chosen to give up one's life. Living in God's order is to live in the Spirit and be granted the fruits of the Spirit. Failure is our inheritance if we try to live this order with man's tools. We must see things with God's eyes and not man's eyes.

An understanding of submission is not easily attained. Many sincere women have labored under a limited understanding of submission. Thus, they were willing to be submissive as long as their husbands exercised headship in the way they desired. Many others have given credence to headship but explained, "Because of my husband's problems, it won't work for us." Others may think they are accepting headship. However, they fight (rather than discuss) each decision. When he eventually abdicates, she says, "Submission is such a wonderful and protective way to live. I suggest alternatives and if my husband accepts them, I have the satisfaction of knowing I am truly living under the umbrella of his protection." In bludgeoning him she emasculates her husband and punctures the umbrella so full of holes that she is left out in the rain.

Even the couple who strives to perfect an equalitarian relationship and recognizes the need for leadership will inevitably find times when consensus does not bring decisions. At these times a husband may have to make a decision with which his wife does not concur. However, if the husband is truly exercising Christ-like leadership, his wife can be assured that he is doing what he thinks best, that he has prayed about his decision, and that he is truly guided by the Spirit. It will not be difficult for her to accept his decision if she is reassured that he is responsibly exercising his role as leader. Basically, the couple who is committed to making prayerful decisions is committed to discerning God's will for them.

On other occasions a husband may decide to do as his wife suggests. He may object to something with a strength of four while his wife favors it with a strength of ten. Because of the trust factor, he realizes, "Susan would never deliberately do something harmful to us. For her to feel this strongly about something must mean it is the right way to go."

Couples may now see the interrelationship of the IT'S and DIS. As decisions are made cooperatively, the sense of interdependence, trust, and surrender is strengthened. So, IT'S makes DIS possible and DIS helps IT'S. An understanding of equality, decision-making, and authority in marriage requires discussion, an openness to looking at life in a Christian way, and sincere prayer that the Spirit will reveal the Father's will.

10

MONEY MATTERS IN MARRIAGE

VALUES AND EMOTIONAL NEEDS

Couples should distinguish between *financial problems* and *conflicts over finances.* A financial problem implies that a couple faces a fairly logical problem to which there is a rational solution. That is, the simple availability of more cash or the wiser use of resources will solve the problem. A financial problem implies finding a rational and logical solution to it.

However, a financial conflict suggests that disagreement is caused by a conflict over values or some underlying emotional need. A financial conflict is more complicated and subtle than a financial problem. In most instances one can only understand a financial conflict when one understands a couple's unconscious emotional needs and/or their value system. Neither unlimited financial resources nor knowledge about the use of money will help the couple solve a financial conflict. Before the dilemma can be solved they must understand their emotional needs and basic values.

Prior to suggesting that couples discuss financial matters and begin to work on a budget, it is necessary that they discuss their value of money. For instance, a couple must decide to emphasize the accumulation of money to buy beyond their needs, to accumulate money to pile up wealth, or to spend money to provide the basic necessities of life. Frequently, couples who explain that they are experiencing financial problems are really experiencing financial conflicts. That is, they disagree over what money means to them.

For instance, a couple may come to a marriage counselor complaining of a sense of "dis-ease" or alienation between them. As they describe their life situation, the counselor becomes aware that the husband is working two full-time jobs and his wife has a job outside the home. Their contact with each other may be limited to passing in the driveway, writing notes, and quick telephone calls. Because of different work schedules, weeks may go by before they have an opportunity to talk face to face with each other. If money and the accumulation of material goods is of the utmost importance, they will need to accept a marriage in which there is an absence of closeness.

Another husband may complain to a counselor that he feels his wife only regards him as a meal ticket. When one spouse encourages the other to work an extra job so they can buy a larger home or get another car, they must decide between the meaning of their relationship, material goods, and keeping up with the Joneses.

Our Needs Are Endless

A couple is eventually confronted with the law of insatiable needs. That is, as our income increases arithmetically, our expenses increase geometrically. Just as we get an increase in salary, we develop another set of needs. During the first couple years of our marriage, Alice was employed as a nurse and I was going through graduate school by the sweat of my *Frau*. We had a fraction of the income compared to what we later earned. Yet, we saved money and lived comfortably. After I completed school and our income increased, we developed several new needs and it seemed impossible to save money. We finally had to recognize that we probably would never have enough money. The best solution to the problem revolved around reducing our needs. Many troubled couples explain to counselors, "All was fine until we started earning more money than we needed."

When a couple begins to grip the law of insatiable needs, they recognize the counterproductivity of exerting an inordinate effort to obtain the comforts of life when these comforts create so much discomfort. It is interesting to talk with couples about how their life has changed over the years. Many have shared our experience and nostalgically recall the years they struggled together, having only money for the necessities of life. After college or some promotion, they got "on their feet financially." After a few years of financial and business success, they began to realize the impact of the law of insatiable needs. They eventually faced the painful admission that the accumulation of goods, exotic vacations, and a finer wardrobe did not make them happier. We are so conditioned to think that we can buy happiness, that it is painful to admit that many of the material luxuries do not bring happiness. A couple begins to confront reality when they admit that they were happier when they had less of the "good things of life."

MONEY AS POWER

Couples need also to understand the power that is associated with money. When they are hassling over money, they usually find that additional cash will not solve the basic hassle. Subconsciously, they are involved in a power struggle which no amount of money will solve. They continue arguing over money because the one who determines its use maintains the power. For instance, the husband who argues that his wife is not giving him a large enough allowance does not have a financial problem. Instead, he is involved in a power struggle in which his wife exerts control by not giving him the money he wants. He, in turn, demands more money as a way of resisting her control. On the other hand, a homemaker may complain that her husband's income is too low to provide her enough money to effectively manage the household. This may either reinforce any feelings of inadequacy he has, or the husband may be denying her money to exercise his control.

People are frequently concerned about the effect a job loss or an economic recession has upon marriage. Essentially, the strong marriage will survive something as traumatic as a job loss or a severe reduction in income. In the weaker marriage where a couple is involved in a power struggle, the loss of a job or income provides the spouses with an additional opportunity to attack each other. For instance, the wife may attack her husband for not finding a job, and a husband may attack his wife for not adequately budgeting the family finances or for having made mistakes in the past. It would be futile to talk with this couple about family budgeting until they recognize their basic power struggle.

Money also presents a problem for the couple for whom it represents security. The one spouse may want to control the money so as to exert power. Another spouse may want to accumulate money to nurse feelings of insecurity. Again, one is confronted with the reality of insatiable demands. The car, the house, and the redecorating will never be grand enough. One man who was very proud of his new $15,000 car explained that General Motors guaranteed that its color was exclusive. One can only feel sympathy for a man whose sense of worth is wrapped up with an exclusive color code for his car. The person who attempts to solve security problems by accumulating material goods only faces failure. Disagreements about priorities generally cannot be understood until a couple understands their values, the investment in them, or their own unconscious emotional needs.

Because of a distorted sense of the value of money, couples easily fall into the trap of trying to keep up with the Joneses. If the Joneses have a new car or living room set, the O'Briens may want to get something better so they can feel superior to the Joneses. It is unfortunate that we often fail to look for the internal beauty of people. That is, we fail to appreciate their humbleness, generosity of spirit, willingness to sacrifice, honesty, and integrity.

What Do We Need?

It is necessary for couples to distinguish between necessities, the nice-to-have items, and the luxuries. A basic amount of money is needed for the essentials of life, such as food, clothes, shelter, education, and transportation. One engaged couple realized the need for money when they walked up the front steps of the parsonage and overheard their pastor and his wife having a slightly heated discussion over the high cost of living. As she answered their interrupting knock, the usually shy wife commented, "He can't see why I can't feed the multitude with two fishes and five loaves of bread." Couples should carefully examine their lives to identify how quickly luxuries become nice-to-have items and then necessities. Is it true that whether one defines a particular item as a necessity or luxury may depend more upon values than upon an objective criteria? The first rule of wise financial management is to save something for a rainy day; the second is to distinguish between light sprinkles and heavy showers.

Couples should talk about their life goals and expectations of marriage. As they discuss what they expect from life, they will naturally begin to talk about the money they need. When couples discover they have different values and needs for money, they should not undermine these differences. They should recognize that because of these differences people identify money as a principal problem in marriage. It is difficult to identify complicated emotional needs, such as power or security. Yet, if couples find that seemingly endless discussion does not resolve differences about priorities or budgeting, they may be quite certain they are either involved in a power struggle, they look to money to solve a basic security problem, or they have a misdirected sense of values.

JOB SECURITY

One basic difficulty many young couples experience revolves around their marrying when one or both partners are beginning a new job. They may tend to operate upon the premise, "I've got to work hard now to establish and secure myself for the future." Consequently, there is a tendency to neglect the marriage. The underlying thought is that the marriage will always be there and one will get around to caring for it once financial and job security has been achieved. In most instances the motivation of the spouse is unquestioned. That is, the spouse has a sincere desire to create a happy and successful marriage and believes that financial and job security is a prerequisite. Unfortunately one cannot set the marriage on the back burner, anticipating taking care of it some five or ten years down the road.

Although it is true that one must work hard to become established in a particular job, one should not neglect marriage and family responsibilities to obtain job security. Disagreement about work and family responsibilities is a common dilemma experienced by newly married couples. As a couple discusses this problem, they may discover that one spouse places an undue emphasis upon work. This person, in reality, may prefer work to marriage, operating upon the premise of job first and marriage second. Although I may not agree with their values, it may "work out" for a couple to place an emphasis upon earning money as long as they do not also expect to develop a rewarding and satisfying life as a couple. But, they will experience serious difficulty when one emphasizes developing an enjoyable married life and the other accumulating wealth.

THE NITTY-GRITTY

As couples think about discussing something as nitty-gritty as a budget, they may consider the remarks of the Italian physician Montagazza:

> To drink from the eyes of a woman who is a perfect fountain of delight,
> To feel the doors of paradise open to us by her lips;
> And then all at once to be obliged to speak of income amidst such intoxicating pleasures;
> It is hard, cruel, abominable — but it is necessary.

In the musical "Porgy and Bess," Porgy sings, "I got plenty o' nothin', and nothin's plenty for me," but even he loses his woman in the next act. Couples should anticipate their expenses, predict their income, and discuss how to divide and utilize this income. Some expenses to consider are rent, car upkeep and operation, insurance, food, clothing, recreation, savings, medical, etc. Of course, different couples have different expenses and incomes, so one can only suggest some fundamental ideas about budgeting. Each couple has to develop its own basic budget. Keep in mind, however, that two can live as cheaply as one only if one starves.

It is most important for couples to budget so they will be aware of how much money they need, where it is going, and where it has gone. Most couples are surprised that they can nickel and dime themselves to death. Frequently, in the middle of a pay period, a couple wonders, "Where did all the money go?" As they think about the major expenses, these nowhere equal the money spent. However, as they add what was spent for lunch, donations, cigarettes, parking, etc., they suddenly realize where all the money disappeared. The accountability of a budget also helps a couple learn an overall sense of discipline.

It is wise for an engaged couple to contact a reliable insurance agent to develop a realistic insurance plan. The "friendly neighborhood banker" is another resource couples frequently overlook. A banker can offer several helpful suggestions about banking services which people may not know about. Other than establishing a checking and savings account, a couple may need to borrow money from a bank. As they make payments on furniture and other initial expenses, they should be aware that the interest rate charged by a bank is usually less than the carrying charge of a store.

Couples should recognize how much interest is paid through carrying charges. Although this varies according to state law, the rate may range from 12 to 18 percent per year. A couple may end up paying almost as much in interest as the original cost of the item. A couple should be leery of easy time payment plans. It seems so easy to think of paying only $10 down and $10 a month. Trying to sell a housewife a home freezer, a salesman pointed out, "You can save enough on your food bills to pay for the freezer." "Yes, I know," the woman agreed, "but you see, we're paying for our car on the car fare we save. Then, we're paying for our washing machine on the laundry bills we save, and we're paying for the house on the rent we're saving. We just can't afford to save any more right now." In order to avoid the trap of impulse purchases, it is helpful to want something for three months before making the purchase.

It is also a good idea for a couple to check with the local credit bureau to discover their credit rating. If they lack a rating or if it is undesirable, they could check with the credit bureau, bank, or a department store credit manager to determine the best way to establish or improve their rating.

Although credit and time payments are an integral part of American life, no commandment says that couples must charge their purchases. Credit and time payments appeal to impulse buyers and are based upon the principle of instant gratification — "Thou must not have any unmet needs." In some cases, of course, an emergency may make it necessary for a couple to charge or borrow money. Thus, it is desirable to have an established credit rating and a pair of well-advised charge accounts. A couple can establish a desirable credit rating by charging a few items and then paying for them before the carrying charge is assessed.

If the couple is entering a Christian marriage, the woman usually assumes the same last name as her husband. She will need to change her name on official papers, bank accounts, charge accounts, driver's license, etc. Some women avoid confusion by using their maiden name as a middle name until everything has been changed and people are accustomed to the new name.

It is also prudent for a couple to consult an attorney concerning the advisability of a will. Generally, in the initial stages of marriage when there are nominal assets and no children, this is a very simple project. A will can normally be drafted which will not have to be changed until there is a substantial change in either the circumstances or assets of the parties. The will can generally even be composed so that the birth of children will not necessitate an amendment, which in legal terms is called a codicil. It may be that the attorney will merely advise that a will is an unnecessary expense and that the assets can be managed properly by placing them in joint tenancy. An attorney can advise a couple of the advantages and disadvantages of holding property in joint tenancy. As laws vary from state to state, however, it is best to consult an attorney to determine what is best in each instance. If the marriage is between persons with substantial assets, it is always prudent to consult an attorney prior to the marriage.

As a couple is furnishing their first apartment or home, they may find it economical to look for sales and opportunities to buy used furniture. A combination of alertness to bargains, imagination, and elbow grease can provide inexpensive furniture and accessories of which a couple will be very proud.

A couple should consider some simple suggestions for dealing with money:

1. Work as a team. The person best qualified to handle the finances should do so, but each should have some designated financial responsibility.

2. Both husband and wife should know how much money exists, where it comes from, and where it goes. Generally, it is best not to operate upon a system of *your* money, *my* money, and *our* money. This contradicts the sense of oneness. All money should be looked at as "our" money. But, it is advisable for each person to have what is popularly referred to as "mad money," for which one need not necessarily account to the other.

3. Couples should have a budget.

4. Use a grocery list while shopping. In a supermarket it is all too easy to pick up items on impulse. It is unwise to shop when hungry!

5. A couple should have two or three months' salary set aside for emergencies. Although it is advisable to have money on hand, it may be well to save for something rather than to save only for the sake of saving. Saving money can become a phobia. Some people develop a phobic fear of being broke and save without ever really knowing why.

6. If you want to become bankrupt, spend more than you earn!

Consider financial and budget problems versus values. Some couples have honest to goodness financial problems in which there is not enough income to provide the basic necessities of life, and others have honest to goodness budget problems caused by not creatively using their resources and defining their needs. Couples with financial-budget problems can profit from a course in home economics — purchasing, food preparation, household care and repair, creative buying, etc. Also, do not undermine the importance of having basic information about money management. However, it is unproductive to spend time learning and talking about marketing and budgeting if the underlying problem revolves around values or emotional needs.

CHRISTIAN VALUES

An engaged couple serious about the prospect of Christian marriage should also discuss what God has to say about how they use money. All we have God has loaned to us. A Christian couple should make prayerful decisions about purchasing goods, establishing priorities, and using resources. This may be their prayer:

For Those With Money Problems

Father,
Your Son told us to consider
The lilies of the field.
But it's hard not to worry
When the rent comes due
Just at income tax time.

Teach us to use our income responsibly.
Show us how to share
What has been given us
With those who have a lot less.
Drive home to us what Jesus meant
When He said to lay up treasures
Where neither rust nor moth can destroy.
Amen.

The Christian couple should understand the frequently distorted comment, "Money is the root of all evil." Money only becomes the root of evil when we make it a god. Scripture tells us that God does not want anything to replace him in our lives. Anything that becomes more important than God is a source of evil. For many, professional football, hunting, fishing, golf, bridge, drinking, or work is the root of evil, preoccupying their lives and destroying the quality of their marriage and family life. If it totally preoccupies them, causing them to excuse themselves from various Christian obligations, such as the proper rearing of a family, it is certainly evil. We often distort the principle of working, playing, and praying by worshiping our work, working at our play, and playing at our prayer.

Perhaps it must also be said that even religion can become a god. Some become so wrapped up in the "pseudo practice" of religion that they neglect their basic responsibilities. They become so involved in prayer meetings and "Christian action" that they forget their families.

What Is Important?

St. Luke reminds us of the place of worldly possessions when he tells Jesus' parable on the rich man and the harvest. Jesus said:

There was rich man who had a good harvest. "What shall I do?" he asked himself. "I have no place to store my harvest. I know!" he said, "I will pull down my grain bins and build larger ones. All my grain and my goods will go there. Then I will say to myself: You have blessings in reserve for years to come. Relax! Eat heartily, drink well. Enjoy yourself." But God said to him, "You fool! This very night your life shall be required of you. To whom will all this piled-up wealth of yours go?" That is the way it works with the man who grows rich for himself instead of growing rich in the sight of God (Luke 12:16-21).

FOR DISCUSSION

1. Have you chosen a secular, rather than Christian, model for your identity?

2. Have you experienced any antagonism toward home-making as a career?

3. Are the differences other than physical between men and women only a function of culture or has God truly created us as different but equal people whose differences are complementary?

4. Have you fallen into the trap of relating competitively?

5. What are your ideas about the need for interdependence, trust, and surrender? Is there anything in your own background, your commitment to doing things your own way, or your involvement in popular social movements that would interfere with the development of interdependence, trust, and surrender?

6. Does it seem that a sense of IT'S is necessary for a couple to make effective decisions, relate intimately, and establish a meaningful sexual relationship?

7. Does it seem feasible for persons involved in an equalitarian relationship to still have one party recognized as the head of the family?

8. How would you implement a cooperative system of decision-making?

9. What is the distinction between financial problems and conflicts over finances?

10. Have you already personally experienced the law of insatiable needs?

11. Do you plan to keep your money in common, or will you have *my* money, *your* money, and *our* money?

12. Do Christian principles say something about how we should use *our* money?

13. Prepare a budget listing your expenses and re-sources?

SUGGESTIONS FOR READING

Christenson, Larry. *The Christian Family*. Minneapolis: Bethany Fellowship, 1970.
   Includes a description of the authority God intends within marriage.

Girzaitis, Loretta. *Listening: A Response Ability*. Winona, MN: St. Mary's College Press, 1972.
   Describes the importance of listening to the unique sound of each person.

Lederer, William J., and Jackson, Don D. *The Mirages of Marriage*. New York: W. W. Norton & Co., Inc., 1968.
   An incisive analysis of marriage in America.

Quesnell, John G. *Marriage: A Discovery Together*. Notre Dame, IN: Fides Publishers, Inc., 1974.
   Suggests how couples can improve their communication.

Reik, Theodor. *Listening with the Third Ear*. New York: Pyramid Books, 1948.
   An account of the inner experiences of a psychoanalyst.

Rutledge, Aaron. *Premarital Counseling*. Cambridge, MA: Schenkman Publishing Company, Inc., 1966.
   Excellent for the engaged, as well as helpful for physicians and clergy.

Denenberg, Herbert S. *The Shopper's Guidebook*. Washington: Consumer News, Inc., 1974.
   Offers suggestions about insurance, medical care, and shopping tips.

Grenby, Mike. *My Darling Dollar: A Handbook for Saving Money*. West Vancouver, BC: J. J. Douglas, Ltd., 1973.
   Suggests how to budget and how to love pinching a penny.

Porter, Sylvia. *Sylvia Porter's Money Book*. Garden City, NY: Doubleday, 1975.
   A comprehensive book concerned with practical money management.

When a couple intends to make a major or out-of-the-ordinary purchase, it is helpful to visit a library and scan consumer magazines which rate appliances, cars, etc.

SECTION III

MALE AND FEMALE
HE CREATED THEM

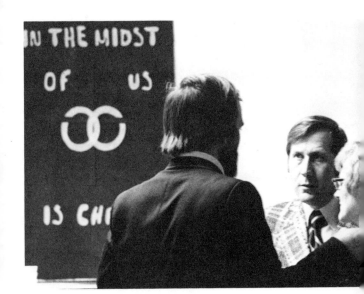

11

ADAM KNEW EVE

For a discussion of sexuality to be personally meaningful, it is necessary to: (1) discuss the attitudes our society has regarding sexuality; (2) examine the different attitudes we have held at certain points in our lives; (3) understand how these attitudes will influence one's rela-

tionship in marriage; (4) appreciate sexuality as a mystery; and (5) understand the relationship between one's view of sexuality and family planning. At one time I could discuss sexuality as one area of interest, and family planning as quite another. At present, I see family planning as so integrally related to one's view of sexuality that I can no longer treat them separately.

When we confront a mystery, such as sexuality, we: (1) might super-sacerdotalize sexuality, treating it as something so God-like that mere humans should not talk about it; (2) on the other hand, we might treat a mystery as trivia. We trivialize sexuality when we treat it as a joke or as just another fact of life; (3) most desirably, we might respond to the mystery by praying to the Father to send his Spirit to reveal what he has prepared for us to understand.

Hopefully, the reader will opt for the third approach to understanding sexuality. The Cycle of Evolution and/or Devolution of Sexuality helps one understand various societal

The Cycle of the Evolution
and/or
Devolution of Sexuality

I. TRADITIONAL JUDEO-CHRISTIAN VIEW

Until 1935 Christianity taught the inseparable connection of unitive and procreative.

This:

    ...Can be embraced

    ...Can be grudgingly accepted

    ...Can be given distorted sense of the sacred
        super-sacerdotalization)

Now we are not teaching in the same age (1930-'60):

    ...Victorian mentality not pervasive

    ...Double standard rejected

    ...More advanced medical knowledge

II. TECHNOLOGICAL TRIUMPH?

(A modified Christian View)

Positive Features:

    ...No anxiety

    ...No abstinence

    ...Solution to marriage problems

    ...No planning

    ...No discussion of sexual life

    ...Children wanted

Negative Features:

    ...Being rigged for intercourse

    ...Side effects

    ...Ideal contraceptive not yet found

    ...Myth of spontaneous sex

III. TECHNOLOGICAL TRAVESTY?

Onset of Devolution

    ...Recreative sex

    ...Gourmet guide

    ...Lack of respect for abstinence

    ...Lack of respect for celibacy

    ...Losing sight of encompassing meaning of sexuality

    ...Lack of respect for other

    ...Best lesson in theology

    ...Parents confused as they see children start at this point

    ...Contraceptive mentality

...Population
...Abortion
...Love child too much

IV. SEXUAL EMANCIPATION

Recreative Sex
   ...Procreative eliminated
   ...Lack of respect for marriage
   ...Extramarital affairs
   ...Nonmarital sex
   ...Canisters of flesh
   ...Playboy philosophy
   ...Free sex
   ...Homosexuals
   ...Re-creative — Recreative — Wreck-reative

V. DEGENERATIVE SEX

   ...Strip joints
   ...Go-go
   ...Comment of free sexists

VI. SATANIC

   ...Nude woman on altar

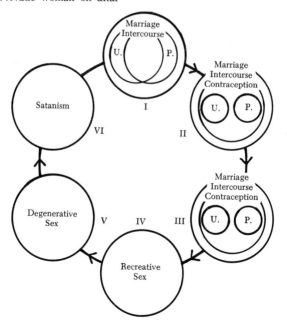

attitudes regarding sexuality, assess the different attitudes to which we have adhered, understand the effect these attitudes have upon our married life, appreciate sexuality as a mystery, and treat family planning as a subject related integrally to sexuality.

THE JUDEO-CHRISTIAN TRADITION

This tradition (Stage I) teaches that God gave us the gift of life as well as the gift of sexuality. Beyond that, he provided us the gift of marriage and, within marriage, the additional gift of the conjugal embrace. In Genesis 4:1 we are told, "How Adam knew Eve his wife." In the Old Testament sense "knowing" is synonymous with intercourse, implying that God intended the conjugal embrace to represent a total revelation of the self — a spiritual, psychological, and physical union. Through intercourse, couples give themselves as gifts to each other — no conditions and no reservations. In Genesis 2:23-24 Adam says:

> This one, at last, is bone of my bones
> And flesh of my flesh;
> This one shall be called "woman,"
> For out of "her man" this one has
> been taken.
> That is why a man leaves his father and
> mother and clings to his wife, and
> the two of them become one body.

God has attached both a unitive and procreative meaning to the gift of the conjugal embrace. In appreciating the unitive dimension of intercourse, couples may pray:

> In this most intimate and private of human acts, we reveal ourselves to each other, we enter each other, we give ourselves away to each other, we join our excited bodies and our soaring spirits, our lives and our being, in passion and joy. In this bed, today and through thousands of tomor-

rows, we dramatize and celebrate our pledge, our desire, our willingness to love, serve, nurture and heal each other, now and forever, for we are truly one.

Couples should also appreciate that the conjugal embrace gives them an additional opportunity to validate each other's sexuality. In an age declaring the non-existence of sex differences, one begins to wonder if maleness or femaleness is of any consequence. At the moment of penetration, the couple accepting God's plan realizes how important it is that the husband be man and the wife be woman.

They know that the validation of their sexuality cannot be confined only to the moment of penetration. The mature couple appreciates foreplay as an integral and pervasive part of the marital relationship. The husband who generally treats his wife as though she is only good for preparing meals, changing diapers, and cleaning the house cannot expect that, at the moment of penetration, she will suddenly feel fully feminine. In the same vein, if a wife treats her husband as though he is good for little other than keeping the car running, cleaning the garage, and bringing home a pay check, she cannot expect that during intercourse he will suddenly feel fully and truly masculine. The loving couple realizes that throughout their married life they must reinforce and validate each other's dignity and worth.

Genesis 1:28 reminds couples of their opportunity to participate in his work of bringing forth new life. Mankind is advised, "Be fertile and multiply; fill the earth and subdue it." This second dimension is the procreative meaning attached to the conjugal embrace.

The Loss Of Consensus

Until the Lambeth Conference of Anglican bishops in England in 1930, the Christian community agreed that there was an inseparable connection between the unitive and procreative meanings of intercourse, i.e. artificial forms of birth control were regarded as a violation of God's will and man could not, on his own volition, separate the two meanings through surgery or the use of chemical substances or mechanical devices. While other Protestant bodies have followed the Anglicans in viewing contraception as not always evil, the Catholic Church continues to disapprove of contraception but affirms the morality of family planning by periodic abstinence. This is not to imply that *only* the Catholic Church has adhered to the traditional teaching. *The Art of Natural Family Planning* by John and Sheila Kippley provides more information about the teaching of other religious groups.

Why was it that in 1930 various Churches began to depart from a traditional belief and practice? Perhaps it was not until the twentieth century that an inseparable connection between the unitive and procreative meanings presented a problem for man. Until then most communities of the world were agrarian and large families were valued. Rather than being concerned about a population explosion, people worried that disease and death would eliminate mankind. However, as the world's communities evolved from agrarian to urban and as medical science became increasingly sophisticated, man was challenged to develop a more total understanding of the inseparable connection between the unitive and procreative and a more functional understanding of the natural rhythms of the woman's body.

To suggest that the Catholic teaching of an inseparable connection has not been enthusiastically received may not come as a shocking surprise.[1] If an engaged couple dis-

---

[1] This teaching is enunciated in the papal encyclical *Humanae Vitae (Of Human Life* or *On the Regulation of Birth).* Issued on July 25, 1968 it is available in The Liturgical Press (Collegeville, MN) publications *Pope Paul VI on Faith and Morals* and *Good News for Married Love* by Fr. Randall Blackall.

cusses this with their parents, they may laugh and say, "Oh yes, that old Rhythm business. We were tempted to nickname you Melody."

The unpopular legacy of Rhythm cannot be denied. Yet, one must wonder if Rhythm and the Catholic Church have been scapegoated. Is the Church all that wrong and is Rhythm all that bad? Or did the unique interaction of socio-psycho-medico influences create a situation in which Rhythm did not have a fair chance? We have found that couples are more open to exploring the value of this traditional teaching once they understand the invalidity of the biases surrounding it, as well as the nature of the times in which it was introduced.

Instruction in Rhythm was introduced in the 1930s and 1940s when our society was influenced by a Victorian attitude toward sexuality which interfered with a couple's willingness to openly discuss their intimate conjugal relationship. A double standard held women totally responsible for pregnancy. In spite of the discoveries of Ogino and Knaus, fertility research remained in an embryonic state.[2]

A VICTORIAN VIEW

Consider how difficult it would be to implement a system of family planning (Rhythm) when the cultural emphasis conditioned a couple not to discuss such intimate details as ovulation, menstruation, intercourse, etc. A repressive education in sexuality was based upon the triple terrors of conception, infection, and detection. This limerick puts it quite nicely:

> There was a young lady named Wilde
> Who kept herself quite undefiled

---

[2] My *The Family Planning Dilemma Revisited* offers further explanation of *Humanae Vitae*. The pastoral and medical implications of this encyclical are also considered in my "Adam Knew Eve: Is It Time to Reassess?" *Linacre Quarterly*, (February, 1976), pp. 238-249.

> By thinking of Jesus,
> Social diseases,
> And the fear of having a child.

Imagine the dilemma of the groom who, on the night before his wedding, was told by the pastor, "By the way, Tom, whatever was wrong up until now will be OK after tomorrow." The couple's instruction in Natural Family Planning amounted to, "Tom, if you don't want more children, sleep on the couch when Mary is fertile." Unfortunately, their conditioning prevented them from discussing these details.

People were reared with the idea that sex was dirty, awful, bad, and were not given an opportunity to understand their own deeply personal experiences. Younger children are delightfully open and naive about sexuality. Unfortunately, as they grow older, they learn that this is something not to be discussed openly and constructively. A thirteen-year-old boy showering after gym class may notice that everybody is not equal. He recognizes that one boy has pubic hair and another's genitalia are larger. Likewise, a girl may glance around the locker room noticing that her breasts are not as fully developed as are those of her peers. One ninth-grade girl, who had a younger sister whose breasts were more fully developed, complained to her mother, "I'm the only girl in the ninth grade wearing hand-me-up bras." Thus, begins a very definite consciousness about one's sexuality.

The feelings developing young men and women have about their attractiveness to the opposite sex affect their perception of themselves and the degree to which they successfully integrate their sense of sexuality into their total perception of self. Unfortunately, in a repressive environment one does not have the opportunity to discuss these incidences and integrate them into one's total life experience.

A DOUBLE STANDARD

Another phenomenon interfering with meaningful discussion of sexuality has been the existence of a double standard of morality, i.e., one for women and another for men. Many husbands were reared in an environment dictating that their sex drive was equivalent to the size of a set of encyclopedias compared with that of a dictionary for girls. Thus, men believed that the woman was totally responsible for the depth of involvement. Within a double-standard society, the man is an Eveready battery who is always charged and ready to go. The woman is an old crank-type telephone which one must grind and grind to get a response. Arousal of women is viewed as a conquest, and self-restraint is her responsibility. The man is depicted as helpless in the face of his overwhelming drives and desires. Thus, abstinence is thought to be impractical for a man, and fertility is viewed as the woman's problem. The martini and the double standard made periodic abstinence difficult. Although a husband might have been aware of his wife's ovulation, the influence of a couple martinis prompted him to think he could support the world. Maybe that's why some children are nicknamed Olive.

Under the double standard, a husband may begin foreplay only to be reminded by his wife, "Frank, this is my fertile time and we did not want number five during our seventh year of marriage." Since fertility is "her" problem, the husband continues the "challenge" of arousing his wife only to find that she breaks down in tears exclaiming, "No, no, we can't." With that he heads for the couch.

In many ways the double standard is as strong today as it was in the 1950s. It is not unusual for a teen-age boy to convince a girl that it is her obligation to have intercourse with him. If she doesn't, he may tell her the sperm will back up in his system and cause an infection. Men also pressure women into premarital intercourse by hinting that their refusal suggests they are either frigid or lesbian.

The influence of the distorted view that the man's sex drive is uncontrollable causes many wives to feel that abstinence is totally impossible. They explain that husbands crawl the walls if they must go a couple of days without intercourse. That men would perpetrate such a cop-out is discussed in a later chapter.

An Era Of Limited Knowledge

It was only in the late 1920s and early 1930s that two eminent gynecologists, Knaus and Ogino, discovered that ovulation connected in time with the menstruation that followed it rather than the one preceding it. As society has changed and couples have become more concerned about family planning, biologists have become more aware of the beautiful rhythms of nature. However, the prediction of ovulation through menstruation (calendar Rhythm) proved inadequate for many couples. Thus, Rhythm gained a very poor reputation.

In many instances, those complaining about "Rhythm babies" were failing the method in that they had intercourse at a time when they might suspect that conception was possible. However, they decided to "take the risk." When conception resulted they blamed the method rather than admitting that they were not paying enough attention to the cycle or just thought, "What the heck!" However, in the 1960s, we became more dramatically aware of ovulatory signs that have existed since the time of Eve. We should remember the Irish quip, "When God closes the door, he opens a window." With proper instruction couples now can know when ovulation is about to occur or when it has occurred through a recognition of cervical mucus, an enlarged cervical opening, the experience of ovulatory pain, and a rise in the basal body temperature. Also, various other signs are unique to different women.[2]

---

[2] John and Sheila Kippley, *The Art of Natural Family Planning*, (Cincinnati: The Couple to Couple League International, Inc., 1975), pp. 22-23.

Although this section contains several references to Natural Family Planning, it does not provide a complete explanation of the method. The suggested readings provide the information couples need. However, most couples find that they can learn the method more effectively and thoroughly by attending classes conducted by instructors of Natural Family Planning.[3] To plan one's family by following the natural cycles of the woman's fertility entails knowing when ovulation occurs. Preparation for ovulation includes preparation of the uterus to receive the fertilized ovum. During ovulation, an ovum is released from one of the ovaries. If it is fertilized by sperm, it travels through the fallopian tube to the uterus where it implants onto the womb. If fertilization does not occur, the lining and unfertilized egg are sloughed off and menstruation occurs about twelve to sixteen days after ovulation.

Natural Family Planning recognizes that a woman is fertile for about eighteen to twenty-four hours per cycle. This implies that if a couple abstains from sexual inter-

---

[3] Information about these classes can be obtained from:

The Couple to Couple League International, Inc., P.O. Box 11084, Cincinnati. OH 45211;

Fr. Paul Marx, O.S.B., Human Life Center, St. John's University, Collegeville, MN 56321;

Mrs. Bonnie Manion, Northwest Natural Family Planning Center, St. Vincent's Hospital, 9205 S.W. Barnes Rd., Portland, OR 97225;

Natural Family Planning Association, Box 250, New Haven, CT 06502;

Serena International, 55 Parkdale, Ottawa, ON, Canada;

Couple to Couple League International, Inc., Twin Cities Chapter, 898 Dawn Ave., St. Paul, MN 55112;

Twin Cities Natural Family Planning Center, Inc., North Memorial Medical Center, 3220 Lowry Ave. N., Minneapolis, MN 55422;

Aware of Greater Kansas City, St. Mary's Hospital, 101 Memorial Dr., Kansas City, MO 64108;

FLIC. Box 464, Piscataway, NJ 08854;

course prior to ovulation (to allow for the life of the sperm) and after ovulation (to allow for the life of the ovum), a couple will not conceive. Natural Family Planning is a system of birth regulation depending upon an observation of the signs of fertility which naturally occur in the woman's body during the menstrual cycle. Several days prior to ovulation a vaginal mucus may be noted. This mucus changes in consistency as ovulation approaches. At ovulation, the mucus is very stretchy and clear. Also, several days prior to ovulation, the cervix becomes softer and gradually opens. After ovulation it returns to its firm and closed state. A three-day sustained rise of four to six tenths of a degree in a woman's basal body temperature tells her that ovulation has occurred. There are also other indications such as ovulatory pain and some signs unique to individual women. One trained in observing these signs can identify when ovulation occurred. Depending upon whether or not a couple desires a pregnancy, they can observe these signs and decide whether or not to have intercourse during the fertile time.

There are two principal approaches to Natural Family Planning. John Billings discusses the Ovulation Method which places primary emphasis upon the mucus as the most reliable predictor of ovulation. The Sympto-Thermic Method discussed by John and Sheila Kippley instructs couples to use the various signs of fertility in combination to confirm that ovulation is about to occur, is occurring, or has occurred. The approach to instructing in Natural Family Planning differs from group to group, depending upon which method the instructors endorse and the emphases unique to particular groups. For instance, some place primary emphasis upon the couple learning the method whereas others teach only the woman. Some emphasize learning the signs and others emphasize proficiency in identifying the signs as well as learning a life-style which permits Natural Family Planning to be a constructive influence on the couple's life.

Since a couple can accurately identify the fertile time, does it make sense, on a purely natural level, to ingest pills, insert mechanical devices, use various chemicals, or undergo surgery, when abstaining from sexual intercourse for about eight or nine days a cycle represents an effective means of conception control? This is especially true when one considers Paul Thyma's citation of the research of Dr. Ruth d' Acry Hart, who found that the vast majority (93 percent) of women *do not* experience the maximum urge for intercourse during ovulation.[4]

I pray that as couples recognize the invalidity of the primary objections to Natural Family Planning — (1) it doesn't work, (2) contraception is more effective and pleasing, and (3) abstinence is impractical — they will be willing to consider the positive value of the Judeo-Christian tradition.

---

[4] Paul Thyma, *Fertile and Infertile Days in Married Life: The Double-check Method.* (Fall River, MA: Raritan Printing Co., 1973), p. 45.

12

TECHNOLOGICAL TRIUMPH?

The second stage of the Cycle of the Evolution and/or Devolution of Sexuality represents the 1960s when man's medical-technical development was such that contraception to many appeared to be "safe" and not too esthetically unpleasant. The general society referred to "sex without fear," implying that man had successfully separated the unitive and procreative meanings. Some began saying, "God, we appreciate that you have created us as sexual beings and we are grateful that you attached both a unitive and procreative meaning to the conjugal embrace. But, we are also happy that we have used our God-given technical skills to separate these two dimensions. In this way we can have intercourse at will and use technical rather than natural means to space our children."

Since the concern about pregnancy had been anxiety-provoking and Rhythm was a relatively inexact means of family planning, the conjugal embrace had been fraught with tension. The introduction of the contraceptive pill, diaphragm, IUD, and various chemicals was welcomed by some as more esthetically pleasant and safe than the condom or coitus interruptus. Many people were relieved that intercourse could now be spontaneous, abstinence unnecessary, and pregnancy planned rather than accidental. Because of the positive features these couples contended with the side effects of the Pill or with being rigged for intercourse. Although the ideal contraceptive had not yet been discovered, many thought contraception was less "risky" than calendar Rhythm. Secular society establishes these requirements for an ideal means of birth regulation: (1) 100 percent effective, (2) no side effects, (3) completely reversible, (4) as completely removed from coitus and interference with the spontaneous sex act as possible, (5) requires the absolute minimum of patient remembrance and motivation.

In Stage II it seems that a respect for life and marriage is maintained. Unfortunately, it often seems that family planning is thought of as only a Catholic problem. Members of other religions, as well as the general public, believe medical technology and "modern theology" have solved the birth control dilemma. Unfortunately, most have been misinformed about the teaching of the Catholic Church, feeling it has told people to "have babies, babies, and more babies." They seem unaware that the Church encourages parents to responsibly plan their families and faithfully rear the children they bring into the world. Also, many have thought that only Catholics have large families. In reality, family size is more a function of geographical location (rural vs. urban) than religious heritage.

The placid nature of Stage II in the Cycle is deceptive. Its full impact can only be appreciated as one realizes that to which it leads.

13

TECHNOLOGICAL TRAVESTY

In the third stage of the Cycle of the Evolution and/or Devolution of Sexuality, one notices the onset of a certain devolution or deterioration. Although intercourse is still recognized as an act intended for a committed relationship (not necessarily within marriage) and although the unitive and procreative meanings of intercourse are still valued, the general society emphasizes the unitive and recreational aspects of intercourse. This is not to deny that God attached a great sense of pleasure to the marital embrace, but recreation was not intended as *the primary* purpose of intercourse.

As couples concentrate more upon the recreative meaning, they turn to gourmet guides for intercourse which help them discover new and exciting ways to titillate the erogenous zones. As increased attention is given to "that great orgasm in the sky," couples lose something of the warmth and reassurance which should flow from the conjugal embrace. Rather than being freed of sexual problems, these problems are compounded. The bride of the 1950s may have sat on the edge of her bed crying (the man possibly felt as bad, but the John Wayne model of masculinity did not permit him to cry), not knowing what to make of the sexual experience that would have been horribly sinful before marriage. It was difficult for her to realize that the body which was supposed to be covered could now be uncovered and aroused. However, the emotional trauma of that experience was less damaging than that of the modern bride and groom who are disillusioned that intercourse is not all they anticipated.

The adherents to this third stage view abstinence with disdain and lose their respect for marriage. Some clergy, physicians, judges, and counselors begin to realize that contraception is not *the* answer to sexual and/or marriage problems. Parents operating at Stage II are aghast to watch their children begin at Stage III. This does not imply that the parents' use of contraceptives prompts their children to begin at Stage III. But, the effect contraception has upon the larger society establishes the type of mental attitudes toward marriage and sexuality which prompt the children to begin at Stage III. Yet, some Catholic parents are obstacles to the effective transmission of the value of the traditional teaching. Because of their own disillusionment, their own decision about contraception, or because of their anger at the Church, some parents do not hesitate to tell their sons and daughters to ignore anyone who is foolish enough to suggest that this traditional teaching has value. Some even become intolerant of the priesthood and the religious life which embraces celibacy.

A Contraceptive Mentality

At Stage III the general pagan society develops a contraceptive mentality. That is, there are some indications that respect for life is lost and that the procreative meaning of intercourse is resented. Some begin to talk about abortion and "populution," a term which suggests that people themselves are pollutants. It overlooks that our affluence, carelessness, and abuse of nature causes pollution. We hear the comment, "I love children. In fact, I love them too much to have them." Hearing this, some people begin to question their earlier acceptance of Stage II. Is there an inseparable connection between the unitive and procreative? Some begin to wonder if they decided they knew better than God and if the larger society is beginning to pay a price for the decision to artificially separate the unitive and procreative meanings.

When Alice and I married in 1959, there was very little discussion about family planning. Since we were both Catholic and had been educated in Catholic colleges, we knew we would practice Rhythm (whether or not we understood it). Within a few years our non-Catholic friends accepted contraception as a fact of life, and many of our Catholic friends decided their Church needed to update its view of sexuality and they began using artificial means to regulate family size. We, too, joined those who essentially made a "non-decision" (went along with the crowd) to contracept.

Within a decade our society moved from a point of debating the morality of contraception to being concerned only with the medical facts of contraception. At present, contraception is an unquestioned reality. It was only in the early 1970s that Alice and I reassessed our non-decision and considered the positive advantages of a method of family planning based upon a woman's fertility cycle.

After having been on the Pill for three years, Alice, at age 35, became concerned about the possible side effects resulting from its prolonged use. Since we had tuned out the teaching authority of our Church, it was no problem to quickly decide that a vasectomy would solve the dilemma. The night before my initial appointment with the urologist, I became aware of Alice's uneasiness about our non-decision. We were involved in only a perfunctory practice of our faith; it had been a while since we had really prayed together, and we had yet to come to grips with our relationship to our Creator. As Alice expressed her uneasiness about our total autonomy, we realized how far we had drifted from Christ and how necessary it was to become reunited with him.

We were gradually becoming aware of the impact of a contraceptive mentality. Our contact with some two thousand engaged and married couples a year was causing us to become increasingly alarmed about the propensity to reject Church teachings which were personally inconvenient. We began to realize how wrong it was to routinely question and object to authoritative teaching. We saw the prideful arrogance that was part of the attitude that "I think for myself, I'm my own person, and no one tells me what to do — especially in the privacy of my own bedroom." The simple concept of obedience had lost its meaning.

We questioned our own crisis of faith and were deeply disturbed about the engaged couples with whom we were talking. As a result we seemed willing to return, with a less jaundiced eye, to a rereading of *Humanae Vitae*. Then, at a critical time in our lives, that encyclical revealed its rich meaning.

Is Spontaneous Sex Spontaneous?

As the long-range effect of Stages II or III of the Cycle are observed, some wonder if "the glories of spontaneous sex" are mythical. Spontaneous sex implies that at certain times a husband and wife are drawn together by some irresistible force. As they embrace each other they become totally intoxicated and are carried off on a cloud of passion to their bedroom. In the midst of their passionate embrace and through the fire of their erotic exchange of kisses, the couple falls helplessly into the marital embrace.

That's all really neat! Yes, it seems that they do, indeed, become aroused and madly embrace each other. The only problem is that one or the other may fall asleep or be interrupted by telephone, doorbell, or children before intercourse is completed. Wouldn't it be more advantageous to anticipate intercourse and plan a time when the experience could be more fully enjoyed? One begins to wonder if an advantage of Natural Family Planning is that couples need to discuss their sexuality, their feelings, and anticipate and plan the times they will exercise the gift of the conjugal embrace. Some begin to realize that spontaneous sex may actually have a disastrous effect upon the sexual relationship.

The obsession with spontaneous sex has opened the door to its being reduced to only a discharge of erotic passion. Spontaneity implies that intercourse depends upon the spontaneous rise and fall of passions. It can degenerate to the point of being only a "sneezing in the loins." We must decide whether intercourse is only a discharge or a true expression of love. An obsession with spontaneity may lead to insufficient planning and emphasis only upon the orgasm rather than the total process of lovemaking.

The commitment to spontaneous intercourse has created a burden for couples. Some of us may recall the Victorian mentality which caused a wife to believe that intercourse was tantamount to rendering the marriage debt. This prompted one woman to confess that she pretended she was asleep on four occasions when her husband approached her for intercourse. The kindly confessor explained that intercourse was not only an obligation but also an opportunity to deepen and intensify the love relationship. He suggested that she initiate intercourse on four occasions to compensate for the times she pretended she was asleep. Given this new view of the marital embrace, the woman discovered a previously unexperienced bliss which prompted her to call the confessor the next morning, exclaiming, "I'm halfway through my penance and I will finish the rest tonight." However, many women who looked upon intercourse as a rendering of the debt were unable to enjoy this "coercive" experience.

In reality spontaneous sex has created the same problem of coerciveness and obligation. Many a disillusioned wife comments, "If I'm going to have peace the next day, I'd better go along with intercourse." It seems that the obligation to have intercourse is one phenomenon causing the increase in the incidence and rate of frigidity and impotence. It is paradoxical that some of the best known sex institutes acknowledge the value of abstinence. They expect couples to abstain from intercourse during their first week at the institute. One might facetiously believe that abstinence would be more favorably received if Natural Family Planning groups charged fees equalling those expected by the secular sex institutes and if they talked about abstinence as a sex technique rather than a means of controlling conception.

If couples plan time to be alone together, they may find intercourse *will* occur spontaneously.

14

WHY WAIT?

Although these chapters are committed to a positive approach to marriage preparation, they also encourage the engaged to focus on issues that may turn around their lives. Most certainly understanding the implications of the Cycle of the Evolution and/or Devolution of Sexuality holds that potential. Regrettably, a significant number of engaged couples have arrived at Stage III to the extent that they have a strong commitment to contraception, a certain antagonism about pregnancy, and a belief that intercourse need not be delayed until marriage.

This is understandable, considering the emphasis of the larger society. I suggest, however, that contraception may complicate rather than enhance married life, even though the practice of contraception by the larger society makes it extremely difficult to suggest that artificial contraception is not the be-all and end-all. It is unfair indeed that most couples are not given the option not to contracept. The assumptions of the larger society cause couples to assume that contraception is, unquestionably, a normal and natural part of life. Generally, a physician will not explain Natural Family Planning and simply asks whether a woman wants the Pill or an IUD. The fiancé is usually not involved in this decision. He may go along with whatever she decides, assuming it will not inconvenience him. The pro-life person must recognize that the IUD works as an abortifacient.[1] Other than this, it is somewhat peculiar that people overlook the complications associated with both the IUD and the contraceptive pill. It seems many people operate upon the assumption, "It will never happen to me." The IUD carries with it the risk of perforating the uterine wall, ectopic pregnancy, intermenstrual bleeding, cramps, syncope, pelvic inflammatory disease, and some less common complications.

It is surprising to hear a "liberated" woman comment, "I have to be sure I don't plan much for the day after I begin taking the Pill each month. I'm always nauseated that day." How is it that one accepts nausea as natural to life? The more serious side effects associated with the Pill are thrombophlebitis, pulmonary embolism, and cerebral thrombosis. Also other serious side effects are thought to be associated with the Pill. Some of the more common and less serious are cramps and bloating, spotting, break-through bleeding, change in menstrual flow, edema, etc. Someone who is more interested in how contraceptives work could consult medical literature such as the *Physician's Desk Reference*. Our society and medicine applies a double standard to the use of contraceptives. That is, other medications that have the potentially serious side effects as do contraceptives are taken off the market or abandoned by the public. Why, then, is the investment in contraception so strong?

Couples who decide to practice Natural Family Planning may receive some resistance from their physician, clergyman, and parents. The physician may comment, "I can't be held responsible for what happens." Many physicians, having

---

[1] Thomas W. Hilgers, "The Intrauterine Device: Contraceptive or Abortifacient?" *Minnesota Medicine*, (June, 1974), pp. 493-501.

accepted contraception, find it easier to prescribe the Pill
than to provide instruction in Natural Family Planning.
Some Catholic clergy may reject Natural Family Planning
as it is now practiced, thinking of it as a remnant of the
calendar Rhythm days of the past. Others fail to see the
moral dimension to the question and look at it as only
another method of family planning. Parents may offer
resistance, feeling they were "burned" by the calendar
Rhythm method.

Unfortunately, people who are very close to the engaged pass up the opportunity to provide them a chance
to learn about Natural Family Planning. They do not hear
the disillusionment of the engaged couples we encounter
who feel they have been betrayed by those denying them
the benefit of this teaching. Of course, some engaged couples
are very angry when someone questions their automatic
acceptance of contraception.

Non-Marital Intercourse

Besides asking couples to question our society's commitment to contraception, may they discuss another sensitive issue associated with Stage III — non-marital intercourse
and living together before marriage.

Unfortunately, many are no longer willing to recognize
the connection between the misuse of sex before marriage
and the difficulties experienced after marriage. It is not
so much that God wants to punish us, but we punish ourselves (unhappiness, marital distrust, lack of sexual satisfaction, etc.) as a result of violating certain spiritual laws.
The couple journeying toward holiness comes to recognize
that moral laws are powerful helps rather than shackles.

Realizing that premarital intercourse has become accepted, and even encouraged, in some marriage courses,
the engaged should discuss their own attitude toward premarital intercouse. One might consider five mental attitudes prompting couples to become involved in intercourse:

1. I call my own shots,
2. A powerful urge,
3. All God has created is good,
4. A non-decision.
5. What's the difference now?

I Call My Own Shots: One rationale explaining pre-marital intercourse revolves around a couple's rejection that God has a plan for their relationship. The couple who denies God's laws governing relationships may be autonomous individuals operating upon the premise, "No one – not even God – is going to tell us what to do." This couple has intercourse because it is something *they want,* and they are intent upon doing exactly what they want. One party may pressure an unwilling partner into intercourse. When one refuses to respect the other's wish for premarital chastity, he or she must question the respect this partner will have for the other's wishes within marriage.

In the 1950s and 1960s it was fairly popular in Christian marriage courses to explain that persons who engaged in premarital sex had less happy marriages than did those who abstained. Simply citing this statistic did not fully explain the phenomenon. It was not the fact of premarital intercourse that caused marital unhappiness. A more important dynamic was the make-up of the personalities. During those years when premarital intercourse was disapproved by the larger society, those who engaged in it were defying both God's wishes and social codes and mores. Frequently, those who defy or disregard morality and social codes and mores are also individuals who experience serious difficulty in marriage. Again, independent or free spirits are high-risk groups. The situation is somewhat different today; it is the conforming individual who may become involved in premarital intercourse. So, now, one may be rebelling against God but not the larger society. Yet, when there is tension between social codes and mores and morality, let morality prevail over social pressure.

A Powerful Urge: Some other couples become involved in premarital intercourse because they find it difficult to control the sexual urge. If they have never discussed the meaning of intercourse or premarital chastity, they may fall into intercourse without actually understanding what is involved. Self-control in many areas is important in marriage. Perhaps individuals who do not pray for the ability to control the desire for premarital intercourse will have difficulty controlling other things. That difficulty may contribute to problems in their marriage.

All God Has Created Is Good: Some other couples become involved in premarital intercourse because they have "successfully rationalized" that sex is good, God has created it, and as long as we love each other, there is nothing wrong with having intercourse. Since they have voiced their love for each other and because they have promised to marry, they believe intercourse is consistent with God's plan, which it is, but only in marriage (Gal. 5:19, Eph. 5:5, Col. 3:5).

One rationalization leads to possible further rationalization of whatever is difficult. It is like lying— it's hard to tell just one lie. Beyond this, premarital intercourse may compromise an individual's freedom *not to* marry. As the courtship continues, one partner or the other may develop second thoughts about the relationship. However, involvement in premarital intercourse may prompt him to believe that he cannot change his mind about marriage. Numerous people have said (although there was no pregnancy), "We had intercourse, I thought I had given myself completely, and I did not feel I could back out on the marriage."

A couple should remember that pregnancy is *not a reason* for "having to marry." Essentially, no one has to marry. Generally, a pregnancy compromises one's freedom to decide not to marry. Clergy and counselors notice that later in the marriage one spouse may use the pregnancy as a weapon against the other, saying, "If I (you) hadn't been pregnant, we would never have married." If a woman becomes pregnant and the couple had *never* considered marriage, it would, in most instances, be ill-advised for this couple to marry until after the delivery, as they would then be more free to assess their feelings toward each other. This does not mean that the welfare of the baby is to be treated lightly. A couple could discuss with social workers the prospect of adoption and their fears about the effect of adoption upon the baby. Some couples have considered marriage but have never actually become engaged. They may think they are just hurrying their decision. It is rather inadvisable for these couples to marry until after the delivery and until they have reassessed their feelings toward each other and their baby. It is very difficult to advise the couple who has been engaged before the pregnancy occurs. The main concern here is that one or the other may fear changing his mind about marrying.

A Non-Decision: Today, regrettably, many couples essentially make a non-decision to have premartial intercourse. They neither decide to or not to have intercourse – they just go along with popular opinion. The non-deciding couple does not discuss the meaning of sexuality. They may feel badly about what happened, but they may not effectively cope with their feelings. This is far too important an act to simply fall into. Some couples who married a decade or two ago made a non-decision not to have intercourse, that is, since the larger society disapproved of premarital intercourse, they simply did not consider it as an option. Today, too often the situation is reversed with couples making a non-decision to have intercourse and not considering the morality of the matter. Hopefully, couples today will examine the morality of premarital intercourse and refrain from it.

What's the Difference Now?

For whatever reason a couple may have premarital intercourse, the common temptation is, "Well, we are going to marry soon and there is no need to change now." Others may say, "It's just gone too far and there is nothing to be gained from changing." Engaged couples committed to this attitude should re-examine their decision or non-decision and pray for the grace and strength to bring their lives into order with God's desires. Whether or not a couple will reassess their position depends upon how they accept God's commandment that intercourse be confined to marriage. If that commandment is rejected, these words can have little effect.

If the couple believes premarital chastity is part of God's plan and if they have been involved in premarital intercourse, they may gain much from praying for the gift of a contrite spirit. It is the mature Christian who can say, "Jesus, we are sorry for having violated the guidelines you offered for our courtship. We ask you to share with us the grace that only you can give and the power to control these intense desires we have to share our physical bodies with each other. We ask you to grant us your grace to delay further intercourse until marriage." This couple will find great strength through receiving the sacraments of penance and the Eucharist.

Couples also need to ask themselves whether getting involved with each other's body and the passionate feelings this causes prevents them from recognizing and developing the other dimensions of their relationship. A total relationship involves the spiritual, emotional, and physical. This is also the order in which a relationship should be developed. A compatible couple shares a common desire to be in communion with God; they have an interest in each other's psychological and emotional life; and they unite their bodies as a sign of their total union. God has intended that this sign of total union (consummation) be reserved for marriage.

My experiences as a marriage counselor as well as my conversations with clergy have convinced me that many couples are unaware of some aftereffects of premarital intercourse. Some counselors have recognized the phenomenon termed secondary virginity, which refers to married persons who have previously been promiscuous or involved in premarital intercourse. We do see some individuals who, within marriage, develop an intense dislike for intercourse. It seems that this is a way to express the anger and disillusionment they repressed premaritally.

LIVING TOGETHER

A full and total commitment is necessary for a successful marriage. To enter into a marriage-type relationship on a trial basis is an unfair test. Many couples who have lived together before marriage find they are as surprised by their partner after formal marriage as those who did not live together before marriage. This suggests that one's behavior may unpredictably change after having made a formal commitment.

Other than being an unfair test of compatibility, one must consider what type of person becomes involved in a trial marriage. It is often a more conservative person who wants to be absolutely certain that his marriage will succeed. Unfortunately, that type of success cannot be predicted. One does not know what adjustments will be necessary or what will happen in a marriage. Considering the more tragic side, a serious accident or illness could occur just after the marriage. The person who needs absolute predictability is a high risk for marriage. The couple committed to adapting to eventualities has a better chance of creating a rewarding marriage.

If someone has been involved in a couple of trial marriages, it is advisable that he or she assess whether or not his or her capacity for commitment has been damaged. When one partially commits himself and yet lives under conditions requiring full commitment, there is the danger that the capacity for commitment will become eroded. A related risk is that a couple involved in a living-together arrangement may after marriage continue to operate upon the premise, "If it doesn't work out, we can still get out of it."

Couples committed to living together premaritally should consider that they are severely limiting their ability to develop the IT'S of marriage (see chapter 9). They are living in a situation requiring interdependence, trust, and surrender, and yet their relationship is based upon the premise that either partner can walk out whenever they believe it is necessary. IT'S cannot be developed within a relationship based upon the premise:

> You do your thing
> and I'll do mine.
>
> If we happen to meet,
> won't it be great?
>
> If we don't,
> Too bad.

15

THE DEVOLUTION

Although the remaining stages in the Cycle of the Evolution and/or Devolution of Sexuality will not apply to most readers, let us consider their underlying philosophy. Such consideration helps a person clarify his or her view of sexuality.

SEXUAL EMANCIPATION

In the fourth stage, intercourse is not reserved for married, committed, or opposite-sexed couples. The unitive and procreative meanings are completely eliminated, recreative sex is commonly accepted, and formal marriage is viewed as passé. Not only is serial monogamy considered mod, but people question whether even temporary commitment to each other is necessary. At Stage III, people believe that intercourse should be engaged in only by those who truly love and are committed to each other, whether or not married. However, at Stage IV, intercourse is not viewed as an expression of love. As long as it is fun, it is OK. Extramarital affairs and premarital sex are defended with vigor and justified as being a part of a new morality. Here the sexual relationship has devolved from re-creative to recreative to "wreck-reative."

Stage IV is exemplified by the *Playboy* cartoon which depicts a guy and gal in bed together with the guy saying, "Let's not talk about love at a time like this." As extra-marital affairs become rampant and as marital breakup becomes commonplace, many a wife has expressed, "That (expletive deleted) Pill! If it weren't for that, Tom would never have felt free to be involved with another woman and would never have drifted away from his family. Many a husband has lamented that his wife would never have become involved in an affair if she had had any concern about pregnancy. This does not imply that sexual mores should be based upon the premise of the triple terrors. Eliminating the procreative meaning, however, causes us to lose sight of the true meaning and value of sexuality. It seems that consequences that complicate cause us to think more clearly.

As people permit themselves to be treated as canisters of flesh, respect for the individual diminishes and the courts condemn to death millions of unborn little ones (United States Supreme Court pro-abortion decision, January 22, 1973).

As long as sex is only for the fun of it, people can begin to talk about free sex. Only a few seem to notice the high price being paid for that which is "free." Free lovers, after a few years, tend to say, "I hate people, men are worse than animals, I detest sex, and I hate myself." The unfortunate followers of the free love movement pain-fully realize that the search for the meaning of sexuality cannot be carried on effectively in a series of non-committed encounters. Some realize that intercourse can only be understood within the protective environs of a faithful, love-inspired marriage. It is distressing to hear the free love advocate explain, "I made love to five women las week." He may have "had sex" with five women last week, but he did not make love to anyone.[1]

The concept of free sex implies that any sexual deviations including homosexuality are acceptable. Since sex is for the fun of it and since God has nothing to say about the exercise of our sexuality, one can do as he or she desires. At this point, some free sexists and observers of Stage IV look back at Stage II of the cycle wondering if contraception was the camel's head. (The "camel head" theory of theology suggests that once the camel gets his head in a tent, it is not long before he takes over the entire tent.)

DEGENERATIVE SEX

In the fifth stage of this cycle the individual is only a canister of flesh. He is stripped of any meaning as a temple of the Holy Spirit who has dignity and worth as a God-created individual. To appreciate the impact of degenerative sex, one needs only enter a go-go or strip joint. After the initial fascination, one is overwhelmed by the realization that no one is watching. Someone is literally "letting it all hang out" and no one cares, no one gives a damn. Some bars which began as topless joints later thought they could make more money if they also went bottomless. They then thought business would improve even more if performers had intercourse on stage. It was only a short step from this to bestiality. Of course, to the free sexist, that is also all right. The above shows the impact of spiritual ecology, a term which implies that as we make a compromise or interfere in one area, other areas will be affected. Essentially, it means that failure to follow God's laws is self-destructive. One begins to realize that "Nature bats last."

---

[1] Some of this material was previously discussed in the January, 1975, *Our Family* magazine, which contains my articles "The Family Planning Dilemma Revisited" and "One Couple Comes Full Circle."

SATANIC

The final stage in this cycle is that of Satanism, in which a nude woman lies on the satanic altar. As we lose sight of ourselves as God-created individuals, we gradually devolve to the point of giving ourselves over to evil influences.

These stages have been depicted in the form of a cycle because of a belief that one historically sees the repetition of this cycle. As we go from one extreme to the other, we are often like the drunk who only crosses the middle line as he is going from ditch to ditch. As the meaning of sexuality becomes increasingly perverted, there is the danger that we will overlook its true meaning and embrace only a repressive view which depicts sex as dirty, awful, bad. This overcorrection has historically distorted the meaning of sexuality. In a May, 1970, address to the Teams of Our Lady, Pope Paul VI condemned this super-sacerdotalization as angelism. This address is translated by Fr. Randall Blackall in *Good News for Married Love*, (Collegeville, MN: The Liturgical Press, 1974, p. 19.). Sexual relations can have a positive value only when sexual feelings are expressed in a manner consistent with God's plan.

16

UNDERSTANDING GOD'S WILL

The reader has consistently faced the theme that Christian marriage stands in radical opposition to the secular world. The discussion of sexuality makes that increasingly evident. You have reviewed several views of sexuality and contrasted them with your own. You have also considered that one's idea of sexuality is integrally related to how a couple chooses to control conception. You have read that contraception hinders rather than aids a couple in their efforts to create a fulfilled marriage. A review of several of the suggested readings, however, would be necessary for a couple to thoroughly explore this statement.

If a couple embraces the traditional Judeo-Christian view of sexuality, they would more than likely also practice Natural Family Planning. If a couple accepts the Christian challenges concerning equality, understands love and sexuality, and develops a spiritual life, they will find Natural Family Planning to be an invaluable aid in meeting these challenges.

WHAT THE INSEPARABLE CONNECTION SAYS ABOUT EQUALITY

The couple who accepts the teaching of the inseparable connection and its concomitant means of family planning would be ideally suited to attack the double standard (in-equality) which plagues many marriages. This method of family planning demands the utmost in communication, understanding, and shared responsibility. The decision to have intercourse must be mutual as must be the decision to become pregnant.

The engaged should also discuss their ideas regarding children and their thoughts about becoming pregnant. The unitive and procreative meaning of marriage means that children are *the fruit* of marriage, that is, children are a fruit of the couple's love and a sign of their cooperation with God's work of creation.

The thoughts regarding the appropriate time for the first pregnancy vary with each generation. Perhaps your parents thought it appropriate to celebrate their first an-niversary with a child. Later, it became "more in" to talk about delaying pregnancy for a year. At present, it is popular for couples to talk about waiting five years before becoming pregnant. There are some alarming implications intrinsic to the "five-year attitude." Couples explain that they want to delay children so they will have an opportunity to get their own heads and marriage straight. There is a real danger that couples will bypass the five-year mark, explaining that they need two incomes for at least another year to finish payments on this or that. It is easy to become accustomed to two incomes, and a couple can become so locked in on themselves that it is difficult to think of living without most of the comforts of a two-income life-style. It is also very easy to slip into a pattern of selfishness which interferes with one's desire to bring new life into the world.

During engagement couples ought to discuss their attitudes regarding children. We are seeing an increasing number of marriages in which one spouse complains that the other does not want children. The other responds, "I told you before we were married that I did not want any children." Premaritally, the unfortunate spouse thought the resistant one would change his or her mind after two or three years. A couple should realize that this closed-mindedness toward a pregnancy generally does not change (For a Catholic couple, openness to the fruitfulness [children] of marriage is a requirement for a valid marriage.).

It is difficult to suggest an appropriate time for pregnancy. Some say that the first child should just happen and a couple should not attempt to control conception at the beginning of their marriage. It is difficult to advise the couple who marries while one or both are still in school. Perhaps a couple should not marry if they maintain an absolute stance that an immediate pregnancy would be "disastrous." Basically, couples should stand in awesome respect of the privilege God has given them to participate in his work of creation.

I *definitely* recommended that couples discuss their attitude about children. Each should *believe* what the other says and not anticipate that his or her attitude will change after marriage. The number of children a couple will have is a decision which depends upon their interests, resources, and what God asks of them. Alarmingly, many couples today are hostile towards the procreative meaning of intercourse and children. A phenomenon which makes artificial contraception immoral is that it attacks that which is intrinsically good — the privilege of corraborating with God in creating new life. That many today fail to see the beauty of new life and the rewards of parenthood is unfortunate. It is challenging to raise a family but it is also richly rewarding.

WHAT THE INSEPARABLE CONNECTION SAYS ABOUT SEXUALITY[1]

Embracing the theology and philosophy of an inseparable connection also aids a couple to truly appreciate love

---

[1] My thanks to *Our Family* magazine for permission to refer to the ideas published in my "Toward a Fuller Expression of Love," (October, 1975), pp. 22-26.

and sexuality. As one can see from the Cycle of the Evolution and/or Devolution of Sexuality, the further one strays from the traditional teaching, the greater the possibility that one will lose sight of the meaning of the conjugal embrace. The communication that is demanded, the greater satisfaction that is derived from the conjugal embrace, and the times of sexual abstinence combine to provide the couple with a greater opportunity to develop a loving relationship.

The engaged couple who accepts this teaching realizes that their marriage cannot be a game of hide and seek — "Here I come, ready or not." Marriage calls upon a couple to engage in a corroborative work of art. A Christian couple is called upon to develop Christian love. A loving couple does not make love; rather spouses express their love by giving themselves as gifts to each other in a totally unreserved and committed manner. The couple who is living love will recognize that abstinence is not a burden but a means through which they grow in love.

The Practicality of Abstinence: Chapter 11 mentions that some couples reject Natural Family Planning because they believe that abstinence is impractical. Here let me say something about its practicality, even though a loving engaged couple may resent the discussion of abstinence, especially the couple who has remained faithful to God's teaching that intercourse is to be confined to marriage. The couple who has struggled with abstinence during their courtship may feel a twinge of resentment as they consider that abstinence will also be an integral part of marriage. Couples practicing Natural Family Planning and not desiring a pregnancy often refer to the fertile time as the courtship (no intercourse) and the infertile time as the honeymoon (opportunity for coitus).

The Double Standard: A certain double standard underlies the claim that abstinence is impractical. Even very well-intentioned people become party to this double standard by suggesting that one should never talk with a man about Natural Family Planning. Instead, they advise one to discuss this with the woman who can then insist upon the abstinence that is part and parcel to Natural Family Planning. Unfortunately, this suggestion implies that a man's resistance to abstinence is so strong that he is unable to grasp the advisability of it. Fortunately, in our work with engaged couples, my wife and I have found that men are as receptive to Natural Family Planning as women. Their self-image is enhanced when they realize that Natural Family Planning helps them control their sexual urge rather than be controlled by it. They also like the idea of attacking the double standard in sexuality by assuming responsibility for deciding when to have intercourse as well as assuming responsibility for pregnancy. When they understand the risks inherent in contraception, they realize love demands that one not contracept. Most importantly, they appreciate more the total love that is required of the couple practicing Natural Family Planning.

Food and Oxygen: The attitude that intercourse is like food and oxygen — necessary for psychological and physical survival — also contributes to the notion of impracticality. This attitude is part of the notion that sex is the *sine qua non* of life. The myth of spontaneous sex is another popular notion which causes people to view abstinence as impractical.

Growing in Love Through Abstinence: Couples who do not desire a pregnancy should abstain from sexual intercourse during the fertile period. Instructors of the Natural Family Planning method can help couples learn to deal constructively with the periods of abstinence. Although they themselves may find abstinence more of an opportunity than a problem, they are frequently instructing couples who have been conditioned to look upon abstinence as a terrible burden. Consider these four mental attitudes toward abstinence:

MAD BART AND BARBARA do not abstain during the fertile period and resent the family planning system which gives them this cross. They may have accepted Natural Family Planning as biologically and medically sound or because their Church told them that this is the only acceptable way to control fecundity. Unfortunately, they fail to truly see the positive features of abstinence. Thus, the period of sexual continence is a tension-filled time during which they do little more than growl at each other, complain about the Church, and curse the woman's fertility.

FRANTIC FRAN AND FRANCIS believe intercourse is a powerful drive which may almost be necessary for physical and emotional survival. Thus, during the fertile time they live mainly by sublimation. They try to stay apart from each other, work hard to drain off sexual energy, and take several cold showers. They may find that softball, bowling, or bicycling effectively sublimate sexual energy. One frantically creative couple considered writing a book describing the sundry ways they found to sublimate.

BEA AND BEN, THE EAGER BEAVERS, see a positive value in abstinence, believing they will realize more satisfaction from the conjugal embrace if intercourse does not become a dull routine. They view abstinence positively in as much as it helps them develop a more exciting conjugal relationship. However, they are fixated on the dynamics of the conjugal embrace and do not see the total way in which abstinence can positively affect their marital relationship. They may clean house, wax cars, bake bread, etc. during the period of abstinence so they will be free to spend considerable time with each other during the infertile period.

NORMAL NORMA AND NORMAN believe that the complete ·individual has an integrated sense of the importance of working, playing, and praying. They look at abstinence as an integral part of their relationship, recognizing that it helps them develop a total appreciation for each other. During this time they control their physical contact with each other. A couple can learn through communication with each other to ·develop a non-frustrating, slower pace of touch and physical closeness appropriate to the fertile phase of the cycle. They strive to achieve the love St. Paul discusses in 1 Corinthians 13:4-7:

> Love is patient; love is kind. Love is not jealous, it does not put on airs, it is not snobbish. Love is never rude, it is not self-seeking, it is not prone to anger; neither does it brood over injuries. Love does not rejoice in what is wrong but rejoices with the truth. There is no limit to love's forbearance, to its trust, its hope, its power to endure.

A couple can readily recognize this as the kind of love which would protect against our propensities to gunnysack or use the silent treatment. Such a love helps couples avoid the senescence of marriage and continually reminds them of the need to be nice to each other. The couple who does not keep a record of wrongs will be unconcerned about who should apologize first. Spouses who are unhappy with evil willingly make necessary changes in their own personalities.

When Norma and Norman are asked to advise people about abstinence, they simply explain that a couple does what they usually do except they do not have intercourse. They have grown together and do not see coital rest as a particularly big deal. They appreciate the many ways in which love is expressed, realizing the phoniness of the individual whose only understanding of making love is to have intercourse. They have developed an appreciation for the dimensions of their love. They become turned on by rearing their children, doing projects around the house, playing tennis, and striving together to grow closer to our Lord. Norma and Norman seek to find the kind of earthly fulfillment which will lead to their eternal salvation.

A Couple For All Seasons: The couple who develops an appreciation for abstinence continues to discover the pleasure of the caressing they enjoyed during their courtship years. The wife appreciates that her husband can look at her or hold her without having to run off to the bedroom.

With each cycle, a woman is reminded that her spouse really wants to live with her and cares for her as a person. John and Nancy Ball have likened a woman's menstrual cycle to the seasons of the year, explaining that a woman of all seasons needs a man for all seasons.[2] They have also explained that a woman often reacts with a feeling of warmth, happiness, and desire toward a husband who respects her fertile phase – all the more desirous of future coital union. During coital rest a man can discover that he thoroughly enjoys the feeling of simply holding his spouse or being held by her. Through exploring other avenues of expression, mutual understanding will grow and intercourse will become a privileged, rather than the only, way of expression. The mature couple finds various ways to convey tenderness, affection, solace, and understanding.

During periods of abstinence, it might happen that a couple begins caressing, which results in an unintended orgasm. If this happens occasionally, a couple may not have sinned. However, if this were to happen regularly and if a form of mutual masturbatory behavior replaced intercourse, it would certainly not be healthy for the sexual relationship, would represent a distortion of the meaning of Natural Family Planning, and would be sinful.

Some couples find ways to make certain that the physical relationship does not get out of control. For instance, a husband who becomes aroused when he drinks alcohol might follow the advice, "Stay dry on wet days" or "Things go better with Coke." If a couple has a sense of humor about abstinence, they can be quite open with each other about their feelings and sensations.

Trust: An appreciation for abstinence can help a couple develop a deeper sense of trust. A husband and wife know that if they can contain their desire for intercourse

[2] John and Nancy Ball, *Joy in Human Sexuality*, (Collegeville, MN: The Liturgical Press, 1975), pp. 51-54.

each can control promiscuous urges during times of separation. The couple committed to this way of life realizes that intercourse is a part of a total relationship and not simply a genital release. They began to develop a deeper appreciation for each other as temples of the Holy Spirit. This attitude, of course, transfers to other people. Because of this view they junk pornographic and suggestive magazines and avoid movies and conversation which debase the meaning of sexuality.

What The Inseparable Connection Says About Spiritual Life

Traditional thoughts regarding sexuality provide an answer to technological and materialistic man who may be prompted to sing "How Great I Am" as contrasted with the Christian hymn "How Great Thou Art." A full appreciation of sexuality leads us to thank God for his goodness and wisdom. The challenge of marriage is more successfully met if we call upon supernatural as well as natural powers. In recognizing their dependence upon supernatural grace, the Christian couple has the opportunity to develop a relationship in which Jesus is an integral part of their total lives. Realizing that he has a place in their bedroom, they may, after intercourse, be prompted to thank God for creating them as sexual beings.

In the previous decades it was unfortunate when a couple would discuss agonizing fertility problems with a clergyman and be told, "Go home and pray about it." First, most of us need to learn something about prayer and second, we need to know for what we are praying. Many couples felt that because they prayed God would decide whether or not a pregnancy would occur. Others were advised that the most effective form of birth control was to pray the Rosary. When they asked if they were to pray it before or after intercourse, they were told, "Instead of!" During abstinence a couple may pray to Jesus for the strength to feel a sense of togetherness. Rather than feeling alienated from each other, they should pray for our Savior to draw them closer together through his own love for them.

The couple who is serious about their prayer life soon learns how difficult it is to pray. We come to appreciate that our fear of intimacy, our need for autonomy, and our fear of change interfere with fervent prayer.

A fear of intimacy is a common problem. We seem to fear intimacy with God as much as with each other. During prayer a couple is completely open to their Lord as well as to the spouse with whom they pray. We sometimes shy away from prayer, not feeling comfortable with the sense of intimacy it stimulates. In overcoming this discomfort we develop a closer relationship with our spouse as well as with our Lord.

Also, our feigned sense of self-sufficiency makes it difficult to depend upon anyone — even if that anyone happens to be God. The development of a meaningful spiritual life helps couples conquer this problem, which is part of the original mistake which caused man to be driven from Eden.

As absurd as it sounds, we often avoid intense prayer because of a fear that our prayer may truly be answered. We may resist the changes that will come about when our Father answers our prayer. Couples need to sincerely pray:

> Dear Jesus, we desire to share ourselves physically with each other, but through the strength of your grace we will contain that desire at this moment and wait until another day to enjoy the gift of the conjugal embrace given to us by your Father. For now, the warmth of your grace will enable us to feel united to each other through the cords of your love.

Someday these husbands will say:

> It started out with you and me, then swiftly moved to us and we.

Proposed that you become my mate, you said yes,
　　we set a date.
Soon vowed to love until we died, it pleased our
　　parents and they cried.
Then two of us became three, we called ourselves
　　a family.
I liked my job, it paid the rent, plus a car
　　you had to dent.
Well, number four was carried home; our son had
　　a sister of his own.
Then came five and six.

We taught them all the Golden Rule, the years
　　went by, they started school.
Once in a while we would fight, but never last into
　　the night.
The kids grew up, they graduated, our babies
　　even steady dated.
So soon the six became a five, (our son had found
　　a mate, you see).
Two years went by and then the five had been
　　reduced to us and we.
But grandchildren came and we spoiled them rotten
　　as ours did to us.
We hadn't forgotten.

As time went on your hair turned gray;
　　as I grew old it fell away.
Eternal youth we couldn't hold, even our children
　　were growing old.
And now you sit beside my bed, our wedding vows
　　fresh in my head.
It must have begun with God above, in a few minutes
　　I'll thank him for having you as my love.

Anonymous[3]

---

[3] Fr. Tim Wozniak, associate pastor of St. Edward's parish, Bloomington, MN, shared this poem with me.

17

THE HONEYMOON

As couples begin to think about, and plan for, their wedding night, it becomes appropriate to discuss the purpose of a honeymoon. A honeymoon provides couples an opportunity to adjust to a new feeling toward each other and to recuperate from the tension and excitement of the wedding.

If a couple truly believes the wedding is a time to visit the home of their Father, ask for his blessing, and ask our Lord and Savior to join them as three-in-one, they will feel the effects of supernatural grace. This will cause them to feel differently toward each other. Perhaps the hymn "He Touched Me" best expresses what can happen. The sincere couple will realize that Jesus unites them in a way they had not truly imagined. The honeymoon provides a couple an opportunity to adjust to this deeper, more intense union.

Couples vary in how they wish to celebrate a honeymoon. Because of the multitude of preferences possible, only a few definite do's and don'ts are suggested here. Most likely, a couple will be very busy during the weeks before the wedding. To marry on a Friday night and leave on a midnight flight for a honeymoon in some distant exotic place is unwise. It might be best to rest before taking off for the far corners of the earth. Since a honeymoon should be a time to rest and unwind, it is difficult to understand why a couple would honeymoon by driving 3,000 miles in seven days. The HALT approach suggests that fatigue makes it all the more difficult for a couple to get along.

It is unfortunate if, instead of allowing time for a honeymoon, a couple insists on returning to work the next morning. Even more unfortunate is the couple who skipped a honeymoon as their wedding was the Friday night of the same weekend that the groom played in a softball tournament. A wedding should be more than just a break from the normal routine and should be more important than missing a few innings of softball.

Other than not selecting the type of honeymoon that will be excessively fatiguing, it is also advisable to avoid honeymoon resorts which advertise wall-to-wall or heart-shaped beds, sunken bathtubs, and the glory that was once Rome. Some honeymoon resorts place excessive emphasis upon the erotic, suggesting that the honeymooners will be surrounded by sand, sea, surf, and sex. This can only set the couple up for a frustrating and disappointing experience.

The couple should plan an affordable and relaxing honeymoon which does not place excessive emphasis upon the erotic. During a weekend retreat with engaged couples, Alice and I had lunch with three couples who discussed their honeymoon plans. One couple proudly explained they were taking a Caribbean cruise and another said they were going to Minneapolis. The third couple remained silent, explaining only, "We're going to West Fargo." After the others left, I commented, "I wish you wouldn't be so self-conscious about going to West Fargo. You're doing something you can afford; you won't have a lot of travel, and you will be in familiar surroundings. Anyway, West Fargo is probably a pretty good place." It's quite probable that their honeymoon did include these suggested advantages. I am surprised by the number of couples who camp. If this is something to which they are accustomed, it may be an excellent idea.

It is also wise to avoid Uncle Ole's advice. Frequently, a couple has an "Uncle Ole" who has been unhappily married for years and who insists upon giving everyone his formula for an unhappy marriage. Uncle Ole usually explains to his niece, "Well, Mavis, you're going to be finding yourself in a hotel room with that red-blooded boy and you will have to be relaxed." He then suggests that Mavis have just a couple of drinks. Quite possibly, Mavis is not accustomed to drinking – especially not on her wedding day. A couple of drinks could be just enough to get her barfing all over the place – not too romantic!

Rather than to heed Uncle Ole, it would be better to demonstrate the ultimate consideration toward each other. On their honeymoon the couple will experience the feelings of having made a total and life-long commitment to each other. Brides often comment that they appreciated when their husbands left the room for five or ten minutes, providing them a few minutes alone. Beyond this, remember, there is no eleventh commandment stating, "Thou must have intercourse the first day of marriage." Several brides have appreciated that when they began intercourse, their husbands sensed they were tense or fatigued, and lovingly suggested, "We need not have intercourse tonight; we've got tomorrow and really the rest of our lives."

In talking about the tenderness and considerateness associated with the honeymoon, a couple can only be reminded of the qualities needed throughout their lives. This works reciprocally – the characteristics necessary for a meaningful sexual relationship are the same ones needed for creating a rewarding marriage.

For some years I was concerned that men were prepared for intercourse before their wives. This involved me in an ongoing argument with God in which I explained, "That's what happens when you aren't unionized. You worked a six-day week and when you came to our sexual responses, you were tired and goofed!" God, tired of this harangue, exclaimed, "Jack, be quiet! Won't you understand that if I created you with exactly the same pattern of response as your wife, you would have learned nothing from or about each other. What is learned during the conjugal experience helps you the rest of your marriage. Similarly, what helps you in the rest of your marriage helps you symbolize the union, in your sexual relationship, which I share with my Son and our Spirit."

During foreplay, the spouses prepare each other for intercourse by stimulating the erogenous zones. The thighs, vaginal area, clitoris, and breasts are the primary erogenous zones for the woman. However, essentially her entire body is an erogenous zone which is very responsive to touch. The penis is the primary erogenous zone for the man, but as they learn more about each other, the partners discover ways in which caressing prepares them for intercourse. The newly married must recognize the importance of tenderness and patience, realizing they have a lifetime to learn this intimate language of love. It is a mutual learning process in which they help each other. Although it is possible that Uncle Ole entered marriage very ignorant about sex, not knowing what to expect, the risk for today's couples is that they may expect too much. Realistic expectation, consideration for each other, and a commitment to learning over time can combine to help a couple experience the union and ecstasy intended by our Creator. Needless to say, these traits should guide the couple from their honeymoon until the day they die.

There is a risk that the sexual relationship may become a dull routine. It is vitally important that couples not fall into the senescence referred to earlier. After a couple months of marriage, a woman may be in the bathroom setting her hair in curlers and looking like she came through a cyclone. As she walks out in flannel pajamas and wool socks (if the temperature is below zero), she may not present a challenge to Cupid. One husband lamented that he gave his wife a frilly nightgown for their honeymoon and did not see it again until their five-year old wore it on Halloween. A husband may just have changed oil in the car and come into the house in a very romantic mood. However, it is wise if he showers before acting upon his romantic notions.

When both the husband and wife are prepared for intercourse, the husband will begin penetration. A couple should not panic if they do not initially experience mutual and/or simultaneous orgasm. For some couples it may take several months before orgasm is mutually experienced.

It is also important for a couple to recognize that some brides will experience a condition called honeymoon cystitis, a mild vaginal infection caused by the irritation of the penis against the vagina. This is mentioned only to alert a couple to the chance of their infection. A physician can effectively treat this condition with antibiotics.

Couples frequently express concern about the length of time intercourse is to last. Answers to such questions must be individualized. Ultimately, the answer depends upon what satisfies the couple. Perhaps it is our desire to be the "better than the average bear" which prompts us to also be concerned about the frequency of intercourse. Again, this depends more upon the desires of a particular couple than upon national surveys. Couples will find that intercourse may be relatively infrequent if they are busy or preoccupied with some particular project. However, if they are on vacation or feeling especially relaxed, intercourse may occur several times in one day.

Couples should also recognize the importance of the immediate time after intercourse. This moment provides couples with an opportunity to shut out the rest of the world and rest peacefully in each other's arms. They should also say something to the other about the meaningfulness of the experience. Just a little "thank you" can be very helpful.

Our Father has attached immense pleasure to the marital embrace. The satisfaction is to be derived from the sense of union that is achieved — a unity and oneness symbolizing the union of Father, Son, and Spirit. As they give themselves as total gifts to each other, the coital embrace symbolizes the couple's surrender to each other. Indeed, IT'S necessary for DIS reason.

FOR DISCUSSION

1. Have you considered that sexuality is a mystery and something that we, as humans, probably do not totally understand?

2. Does it seem that we do, indeed, swing from one extreme to the other and that, for some reason, we have failed to truly understand God's plan?

3. Do you see yourself as open to considering that the emphasis of the secular world poses more problems than solutions?

4. Is there evidence to suggest that all the truth about contraception is not beng told and that information regarding Natural Family Planning his been conveyed in a negatively biased way?

5. Do you see any value on a purely natural and physiological basis of Natural Famly Planning as compared to artificial contraception?

6. Have you previously considered the modern applicability of the traditional Judaic-Christian teaching regarding premarital intercourse and trial marriage?

7. Would you be open to exploring Natural Family Planning and truly seeking to understand its practice?

8. What discussion have you and your fiancé or fiancée had regarding children? Are you open to having children? When in your marriage do you plan to have children? Would both of you continue working outside the home after the birth of your first baby?

9. In what ways could periodic sexual abstinence help you develop a deeper sense of marital love?

10. Do you have plans for a honeymoon? What purpose should the honeymoon serve?

SUGGESTIONS FOR READING

Ball, John and Nancy. *Joy in Human Sexuality.* Collegeville, MN: The Liturgical Press, 1975.

> Suggests the many ways that Natural Family Planning helps a couple grow in their love.

Bertocci, Peter. *Love and the Person.* New York: Sheed and Ward, 1967.

> A philosophical discussion of the meaning of sexuality.

Billings, John and Lyn. *Natural Family Planning: The Ovulation Method.* Collegeville, MN: The Liturgical Press, 1974.

> Explains Natural Family Planning with specific emphasis upon the Ovulation Method.

Blackall, Randall. *Good News for Married Love,* Collegeville, MN: The Liturgical Press, 1974.

> Contains the address by Pope Paul VI to the Teams of Our Lady and the encyclical *Humanae Vitae.* The Holy Father explains very positively the divine outlook on the duality of the sexes, marriage, married love, the marriage act, child-bearing, parenthood, and human love. Modern sense-line format for easy reading.

Haughton, Rosemary. *The Mystery of Sexuality.* New York: Paulist Press, 1972.

> A helpful discussion of the meaning of God's gift of sexuality.

Human Life in Our Day. Pastoral Letter of American Hierarchy, November 15, 1968.

> A statement of the American bishops which directs itself to the meaning of sexuality.

Joyce, Mary Rosera and Robert E. *New Dynamics in Sexual Love.* Collegeville, MN: St. John's University Press, 1970.

> A theological and philosophical discussion of sexuality, suggesting that the full expression of sexual love in marriage has a profound supernatural as well as natural dimension.

Kippley, John F. *Birth Control and the Marriage Covenant.* Collegeville, MN: The Liturgical Press, 1976.

> A discussion of the meaning of the inseparable connection between the unitive and procreative meanings of intercourse.

Kippley, John F. and Sheila. *The Art of Naural Family Planning.* P.O. Box 11084, Cincinnati 45211: The Couple to Couple League International, Inc., 1975. Also available from The Liturgical Press, Collegeville, MN 56321.

> An excellent and multi-faceted description of Natural Family Planning. Comprehensive bibliography.

Kippley, Sheila. *Breast Feeding and Natural Child Spacing:
The Ecology of Natural Mothering*. New York and Balti-
more: Penguin Books, Inc., 1969.

> Explains how the breast-feeding mother contributes to
> her own psychic fulfillment and to the emotional
> security of her child and how breast feeding is a
> means of child spacing.

Parenteau-Carreau, Suzanne. *Love and Life: Fertility and
Conception Prevention*. Published and distributed by
SERENA, 55 Parkdale Ave., Ottawa, ON, Canada, K1Y
1E5.

> An excellent summary of the process of human repro-
> duction as well as the available means of conception
> control.

Pope Paul VI. *On the Regulation of Birth (Humanae Vitae,*
Encyclical Letter, July 25, 1968) is available in the book-
let *Pope Paul VI on Faith and Morals*. Collegeville, MN:
The Liturgical Press.

> In this encyclical the description of the meaning of
> human love is unexcelled.

Quesnell, John G. *The Family Planning Dilemma Revisited*.
Chicago: Franciscan Herald Press, 1975.

> A discussion of the meaning of the encyclical *Humanae
> Vitae*. It discusses the process of making a conscien-
> tious decision in family planning.

Suenens, Leo Cardinal Josef. *Love and Control: The Contemporary Problem*. New York: Paulist Press, 1960.

> A highly inspirational exposition of the teaching of
> the Catholic Church on love and marriage, sexual
> morality, and Christian self-mastery in the service of
> true love.

Thyma, Paul. *The Double Check Method of Natural Family
Planning*. Fall River, MA: Author's revised edition, 1976.

> A discussion of an approach to Natural Family Plan-
> ning.

SECTION IV

BUILDING UPON ROCK

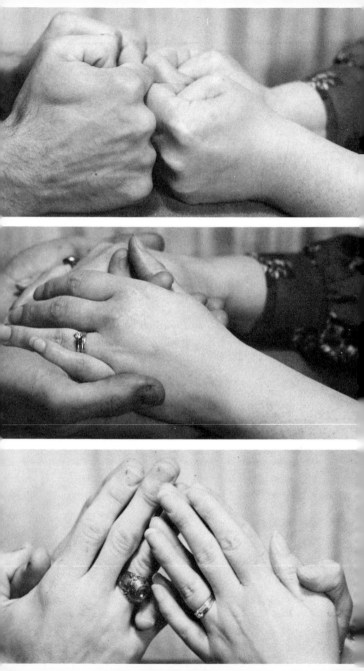

18

JESUS AS LORD

The third challenge facing the Christian couple – to develop a spiritual life – has been mentioned in previous chapters. This challenge involves our willingness to acquaint ourselves with the teachings of Jesus, to pray for the grace to follow those teachings, and to continually grow in closeness to and love for our Lord and Savior. This leads us to a willingness to invite Jesus to be the Lord of our life. Hopefully, many engaged couples will share in the experience of Zacchaeus (Luke 19:1-10) who had climbed a tree for a glimpse of Jesus as he walked into his community. Jesus came under the tree, looked up at Zacchaeus, and said, "Today, I will come into your home." After Jesus entered his home, the life of Zacchaeus was never again the same.

We should pray for the grace to understand our Lord's will for us. As we come to appreciate the difference between his will and the world's, we will continue to discern the unique call of the Christian couple who recognizes Jesus as the model of love.

To understand the meaning of a Christian relationship, a couple might visualize three different pictures of hands. First, consider a pair of hands, each of which is folded into a fist. This depicts the couple completely locked in on themselves. As the hands would knock against each other, so does the couple turned in on themselves knock against each other.

The second picture is that of a pair of hands which are tightly interlaced with each other, clutching and holding each other. This depicts the very dependent couple who draw their basic sustenance from each other. As much as self-centeredness robs the first couple of their freedom, a pathological dependency robs the second couple of their freedom.

The third picture is that of hands folded in prayer. Each hand is placed against the other and is directed toward heaven. The couple symbolized by this picture is the one whose life is Christ-centered. They prayerfully direct themselves toward Christ. They have freedom to move, they are comfortable, and they know what they are about.[1]

The Christian couple is committed to setting aside time for individual prayer as well as for prayer together. The Bible, which contains the master plan for living marriage, has a prominent place in their home and becomes well-worn as the couple turns to it to be enriched by its timeless messages. In their daily prayer the couple thanks the Lord for his goodness and his many blessings upon their lives. They reflect upon their lives to see how closely they follow the light of the gospel. They also petition the Lord to send even more blessings to them, recognizing that the Lord wants to fill the lives of those who walk with him.

Participation in the prayer life of the Church is not a perfunctory Sunday experience for a truly Christian couple. Instead, the liturgical year will be fully visible in their home as its decorum reflects the liturgical seasons. One of the first things the couple does as they move into their new home is to invite their priest or minister to bless that dwelling. Name and baptism days and anniversaries are

---

[1] An insight I received from Mr. Marty Leifeld.

occasions for authentic Christian celebration. Their anniversary provides the couple an opportunity to relight the Christ candle that brightened their wedding ceremony.

It cannot be denied that the Christian couple is called upon to live an ideal life. Yet, the expression "ideal" can mislead one to believe that it is an impractical pie-in-the-sky existence. In fact, nothing is more practical than Christian marriage — if we did not already have it, we would have to invent it. In choosing Jesus to be the Lord of the home, the couple chooses to build upon rock — the way of God (Matthew 7:24-27) — rather than sand — the way of the world. The wind and the rain may come, but the home will survive.

FOR DISCUSSION

1. What does entering an authentic Christian marriage mean to you?

2. Would you consider inviting your close friends and relatives to join in an evening of prayerful reflection to help each of you prepare spiritually for the wedding day?

3. What identifiable areas deserve further discussion before your wedding day?

4. Have you begun to pray together?

5. If you believe Jesus is Lord, what effect does that belief have upon your relationship?

SUGGESTIONS FOR READING

The Bible. Various translations and price ranges.

Only by daily reading of the Bible, can a couple come to appreciate its richness and applicability to contemporary life. Most importantly, it is the way to become acquainted with God and his Son.

Christenson, Larry. *The Christian Family.* Minneapolis: Bethany Fellowship, 1970.

The author helps a couple understand the personal relationship they can develop with our Lord.

Enzler, Clarence. *My Other Self.* Denville, NJ: Bruce Publishing Company, Inc., 1958.

Here Christ speaks to the reader in intimate conversations, seeking to make him fully aware of what it means to be a Christian, "another Christ," Christ's "other self."

Ousler, Fulton. *The Greatest Story Ever Told.* Garden City, New York: Image Books, 1949.

A classic on the life of Christ.

CHRISTIAN MARRIAGE - A Gift of the Spirit is an audiovisual program for couples contemplating marriage. The program consists of six hour-long cassets, six 150-frame filmstrips, six follow-along scripts, a director's guide, and a copy of THREE TO GET READY by John Quesnell.

Other titles of Family Life from The Liturgical Press

MAN: The Greatest of Miracles
The Ovulation Method of Natural Family Planning
Planning Your Family the S-T Way
Birth Control and the Marriage Contract
The Meaning of Contraception
The Head of the Family
The Art of Natural Family Planning
Good News for Married Love
Joy in Human Sexuality

A complete, descriptive catalog of the many titles pertaining to family life in the Popular Liturgical Library series will gladly be sent gratis upon request.

Address:

> The Liturgical Press
> St. John's Abbey
> Collegeville, Minnesota 56321